Key skills for kids
MATH

Let's get started!

priddy books
big ideas for little people

Contents

Answers are on pages 118–127!

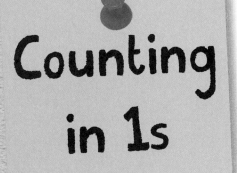

Counting in 1s

We often **count on** and **back** in jumps of 1. As groups get bigger, we might find that it is easier to count in bigger jumps, like 2s, 5s, or 10s.

1 Count in 1s to fill in the gaps to 20.

| 1 | | 3 | | 5 | 6 | | | | 10 |

| 11 | 12 | | | | | 17 | | | |

2 Count in 1s to figure out how many objects are in each group.

.... tickets

.... wagons

.... passengers

What's your name?

Numbers have names just like we do! In math, we usually write their names as **numerals**, like 1, 2, or 3, but we can also write their names using letters.

> Numerals are symbols we use to show a certain amount.

1 Match each numeral to its name.

five	one	3	nine	8
eight	7	0	9	two
4	three	1	2	six
6	seven	four	zero	5

2 Fill in the information about each of these numbers.

	Shade the ten frame	Write the name		Draw the amount
2		....two....		
5		....		
9		....		

Join the dots to 20

1 Practice counting on from 0 to 20, then back from 20 to 0 by joining the dots to complete the picture.

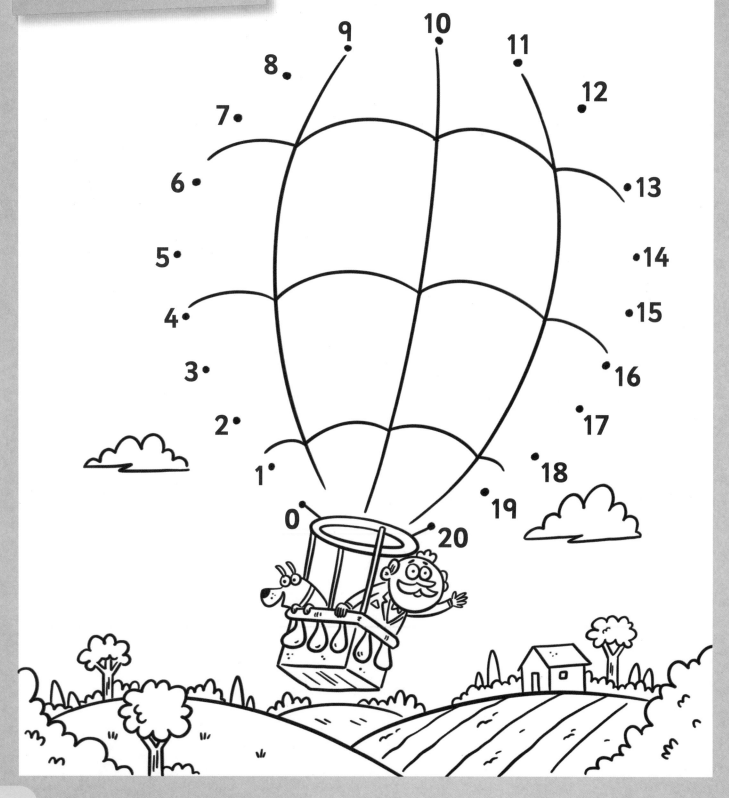

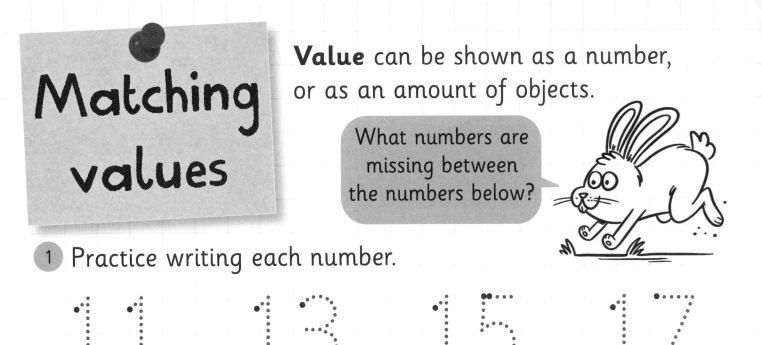

Matching values

Value can be shown as a number, or as an amount of objects.

What numbers are missing between the numbers below?

1 Practice writing each number.

11   13   15   17

2 Count how many objects are in each group, then match each group to the correct number.

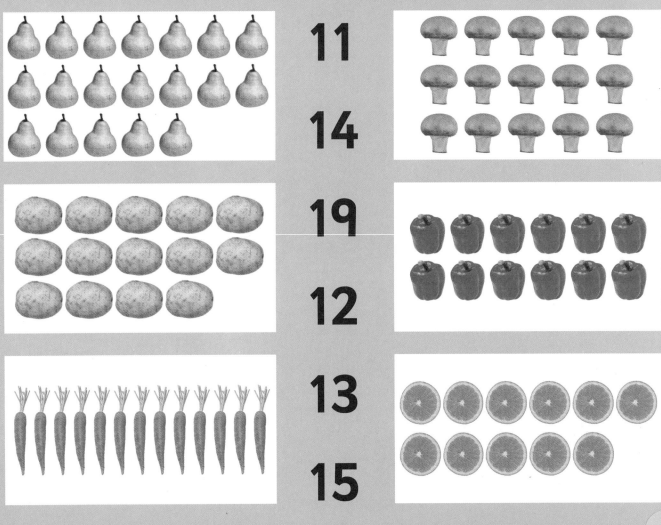

11

14

19

12

13

15

Button up to 20

Numbers can be represented in lots of different ways. Numerals, pictures, or using ten squares are some of the ways we can record amounts.

1 Writing numbers correctly can be tough! Start at the dot to write each number.

18   16   12   14

19   15   13

2 Draw the correct number of buttons in each sewing kit. One button fits in each square. The first one is done for you.

11

15

17

See the example for help!

13

19

Number words to 10

When you can read **number words** from 1 to 10, you will be able to read many other number words, too.

1 Trace each word, then color the correct number of dots.

one   two   three   four   five

six   seven   eight   nine   ten

2 Unscramble the number words, then draw a line to match each word to its correct numeral.

sneve	_ _ _ _ _	**8**
eetrh	_ _ _ _ _	**1**
nte	_ _ _	**7**
neo	_ _ _	**3**
gieht	_ _ _ _ _	**10**

All about addition

152 + 75 = ?

We can use different words when we **add**.

| addition | sum | altogether |

| total | combining |

1 Combine the matching groups to make one large group.

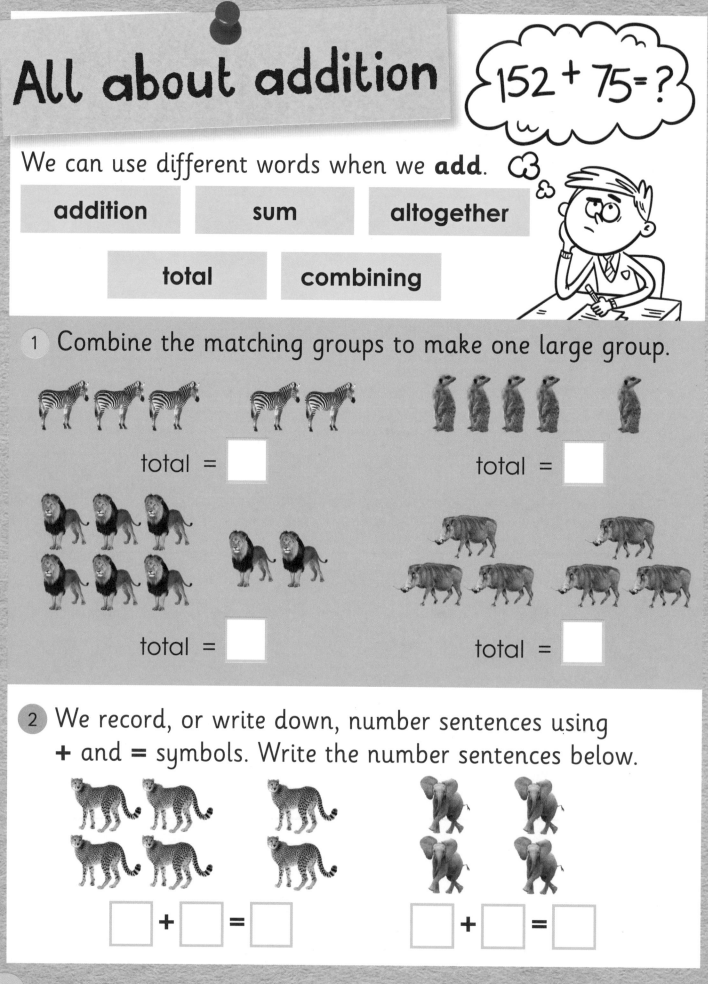

total = ☐

total = ☐

total = ☐

total = ☐

2 We record, or write down, number sentences using **+** and **=** symbols. Write the number sentences below.

☐ **+** ☐ **=** ☐   ☐ **+** ☐ **=** ☐

Times of the day

There are 60 seconds in a minute, 60 minutes in an hour, and 24 hours in a day.

Waking up	At school	Eating dinner	Going to bed

1 Use the word bank to fill in the gaps.

I wake up at **7 o'clock** in the ....

I eat dinner at **5 o'clock** in the ....

I go to bed at **7 o'clock** at ....

Word bank

afternoon
morning
night

2 Read the hands on each clock below, then fill in the blank spaces with the correct time. The first one is done for you.

It is
..7... o'clock.

It is
...... o'clock.

It is
...... o'clock.

It is
...... o'clock.

Finding 10

Recognizing **addition** to 10 helps us to use our number knowledge when solving other problems that involve 10.

1 Use two colors to fill in each ten frame, then write number sentences to match. The first one is done for you.

$3 + 7 = 10$

$\square + \square = 10$

$\square + \square = 10$

$\square + \square = 10$

2 Now use three colors, then write the number sentences.

$2 + 5 + 3 = 10$

$\square + \square + \square = 10$

$\square + \square + \square = 10$

$\square + \square + \square = 10$

Sums to 10

Use the number line to help you.

1 2 3 4 5 6 7 8 9 10

1 Color the sums that **=** 10 to find your way to the roller coaster.

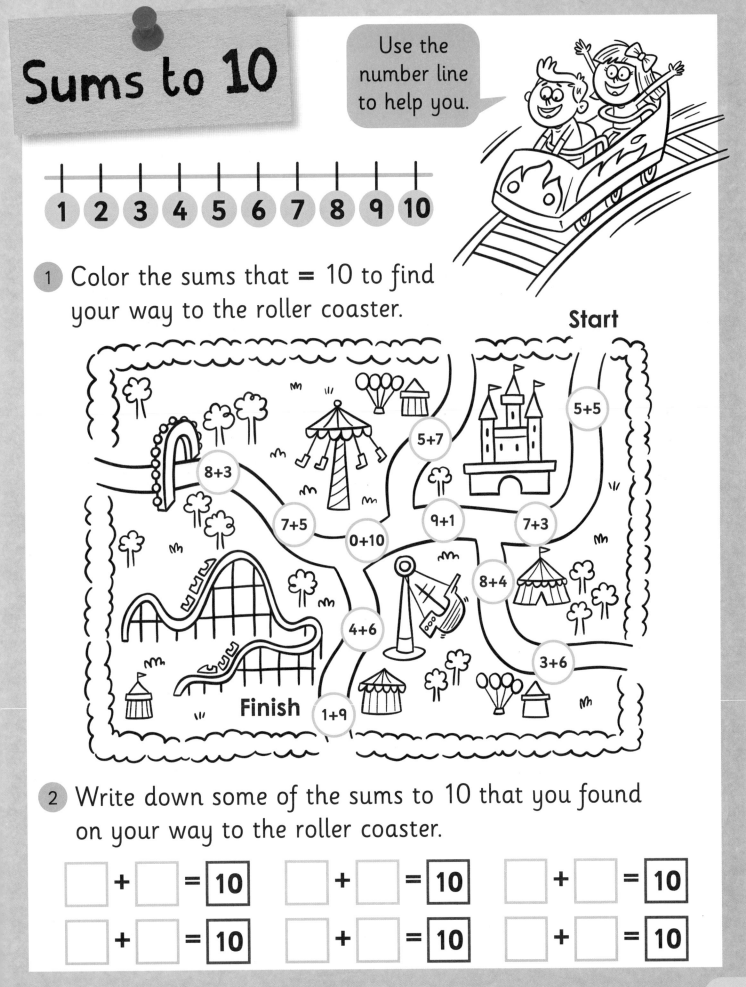

Start

5+5

5+7

8+3

7+5

9+1

7+3

0+10

8+4

4+6

3+6

Finish

1+9

2 Write down some of the sums to 10 that you found on your way to the roller coaster.

☐ + ☐ = **10**   ☐ + ☐ = **10**   ☐ + ☐ = **10**

☐ + ☐ = **10**   ☐ + ☐ = **10**   ☐ + ☐ = **10**

Balance the seesaw

The **equals sign =** tells us when two numbers, or amounts, have the **same value**.

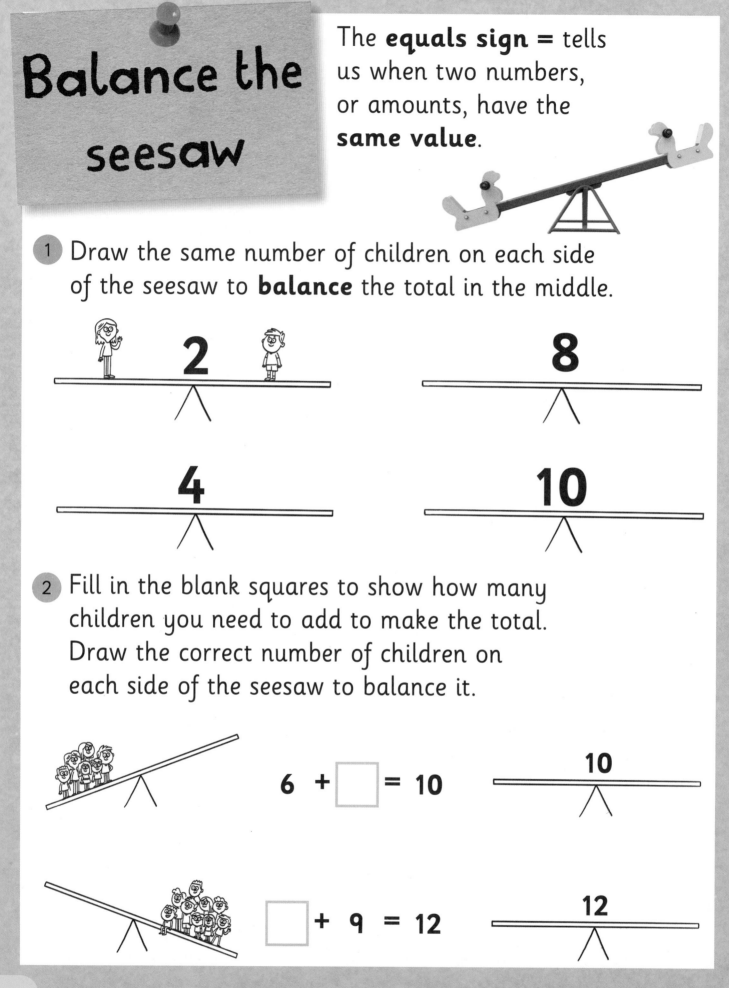

1 Draw the same number of children on each side of the seesaw to **balance** the total in the middle.

2
2 Fill in the blank squares to show how many children you need to add to make the total. Draw the correct number of children on each side of the seesaw to balance it.

6 + ☐ = 10

☐ + 9 = 12

How many in common?

Finding out how many are **in common** can help us to figure out how many are left over.

1. Count how many marbles Jacob and Ava have in common. The first one is done for you.

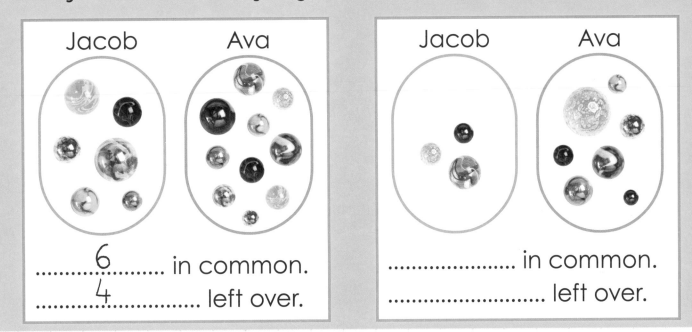

Jacob   Ava

...........6........... in common.
...........4........... left over.

Jacob   Ava

.... in common.
.... left over.

2. Lizzie has 10 bracelets. Her friend Zara has decided to compare how many bracelets they have.

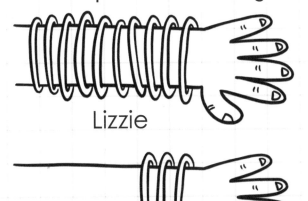

Lizzie

Zara

How many bracelets do they have in common .... ?

How many bracelets are left over .... ?

Find out the difference

Finding out the **difference** between two amounts tells us what information we need to include in a number sentence.

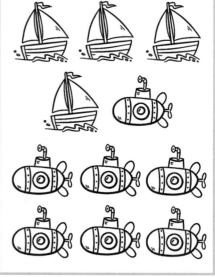

1. What is the difference between six and three?

    6 - 3 = ☐

    You can use your fingers to solve the problem, like this:

2. Use your fingers to solve each subtraction problem below.

    10 - 5 = ☐   **8 - 3 =** ☐   **7 - 2 =** ☐

3. Count the objects and figure out how many more and less there are.

    There are ⎡7⎤ 🚢 and ☐ ⛵ .

    There are ☐ more 🚢 than ⛵ .

    There are ☐ fewer ⛵ than 🚢 .

16

10 out of 10

Use your knowledge of 10 to solve the problems on this page.

1 Use the ten frames to help you solve each word problem.

Kylie had **10** apples. She kept **4** apples and gave the rest to Joe. How many apples did Joe get? ....

Ahmed shared his **10** apples equally with Ben. Ben got **5** apples. How many apples did Ahmed keep? ....

Sam found **10** apples. She gave **2** to Jen and kept the rest. How many apples did Sam get? ....

2 There are two parts to each word problem. Fill in the ten frame, then write the number sentence.

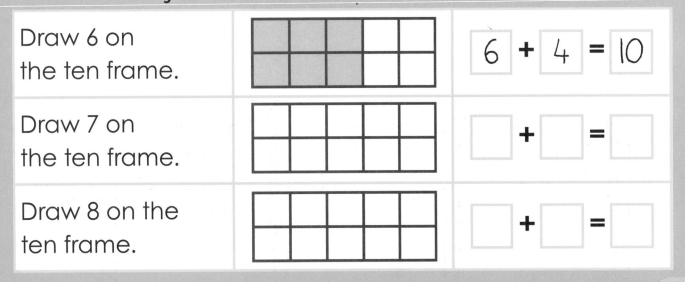

Draw 6 on the ten frame.		6 + 4 = 10
Draw 7 on the ten frame.		☐ + ☐ = ☐
Draw 8 on the ten frame.		☐ + ☐ = ☐

Patterns all around

Patterns are all around us. We see them on our clothes, in our food, and even in math!

A **repeated** pattern is something that happens over and over again.

1 Can you figure out what comes next? Complete the patterns.

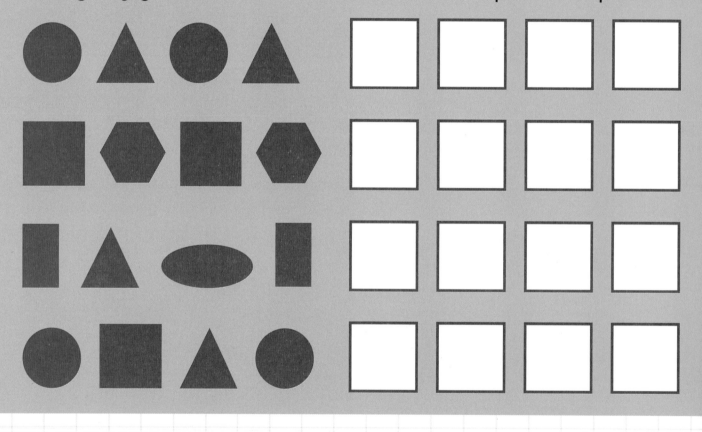

2 Using three colors, see how many flag patterns you can create by filling in each stripe in a different color.

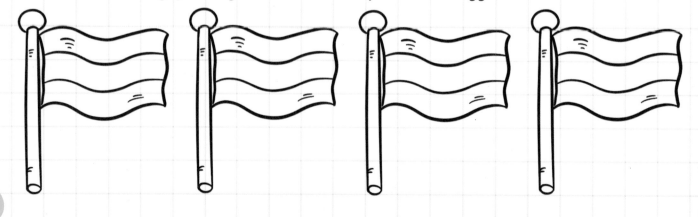

Pattern creator

We can check if a **sequence** is a repeating pattern by seeing if it follows the same rule over and over again. If the sequence does not follow the same rule over and over again, it is not a repeating pattern.

1 Circle the sequences that have repeating patterns.

2 Create three different repeating patterns using the following shapes:

How many repeating patterns can you make from these shapes?

Pattern 1:

....

Pattern 2:

....

Pattern 3:

....

Soar to 12

3... 2...1...
BLAST-OFF!

When we add two numbers together, we can find the **total**. Use the number line to help you figure out which number is missing from each of the problems.

1 2 3 4 5 6 7 8 9 10 11 12

1 Draw the missing objects to complete the number sentences.

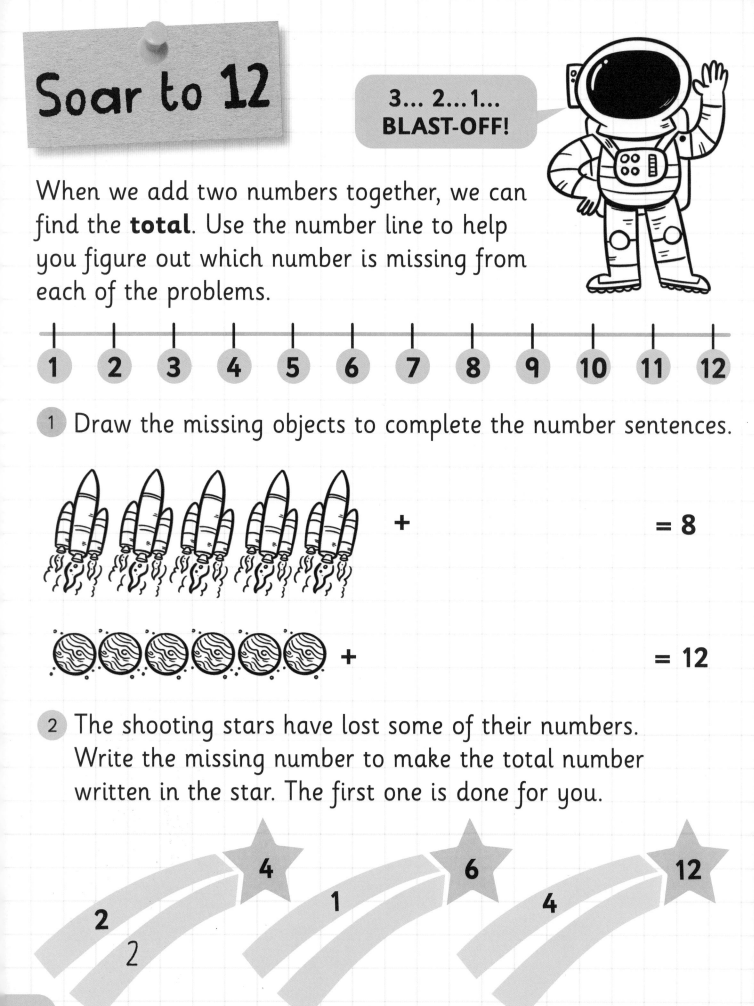

+ = 8

+ = 12

2 The shooting stars have lost some of their numbers. Write the missing number to make the total number written in the star. The first one is done for you.

4

2
2

1

6

4

12

Number ninja 15

When we know lots of information about a number, we become number ninjas who can solve all sorts of number problems.

1. Cross out the groups that do not equal 15.

2. Use two colors to fill in each string of beads, then write the number sentences. The first one is done for you.

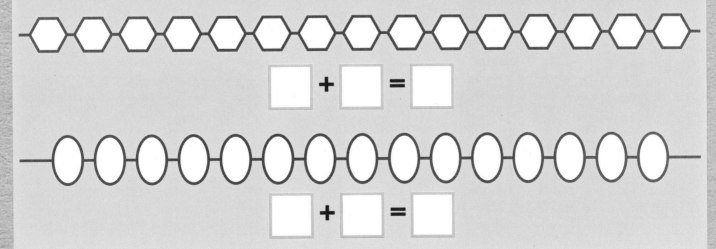

$$4 + 11 = 15$$

☐ + ☐ = ☐

☐ + ☐ = ☐

18 partitioning

Partitioning makes bigger numbers easier to understand.

Dividing bigger groups into smaller groups can help us to learn more about the number we are working with.

1. Break each group into two smaller sets. Write a number sentence to match.

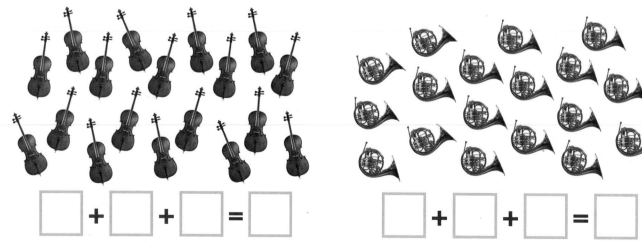

☐ + ☐ = ☐   ☐ + ☐ = ☐

2. Break each group into three smaller sets. Write a number sentence to match.

☐ + ☐ + ☐ = ☐   ☐ + ☐ + ☐ = ☐

2D shape spotting

2D shapes are flat. Looking at the sides and corners of each shape helps us to identify what shape it is.

1. Trace each shape, then draw a line to match it to its name.

| triangle | square | oval | circle | rhombus |

2. Color each shape using the colors from the key below.

How many of each shape did you color in?

circle.............................
oval..............................
rhombus.........................
triangle........................
rectangle.......................
square..........................

2D shape detective

There are some special words we can use when describing **2D shapes**. Once we learn these words, we can use them to sort shapes into categories.

Vertices are corners.

1. Fill in the **2D** shape fact file.

circle	I have..........sides. I have..........vertices.
rectangle	I have..........sides. I have..........vertices.
triangle	I have..........sides. I have..........vertices.

rhombus	I have..........sides. I have..........vertices.
square	I have..........sides. I have..........vertices.
pentagon	I have..........sides. I have..........vertices.

2. Read the clues, then draw a line to match each clue to to the correct shape.

I have 4 straight sides.
I have 4 right-angled vertices.

I have 0 straight sides.
I have 0 vertices.

I have 5 straight sides.
I have 5 vertices.

pentagon

square

circle

Double double

Adding the same two numbers together is called **doubling**. When something grows or increases by double, we are adding on the same amount again.

1 Can you double the amount of candies?
Draw them in the box on the right.

Draw double below

2 Rob ordered treats from the bakery for his party.
Lots of people said they could come to the party, so he called the bakery and asked them to double his order.

Rob's original order

Draw double below

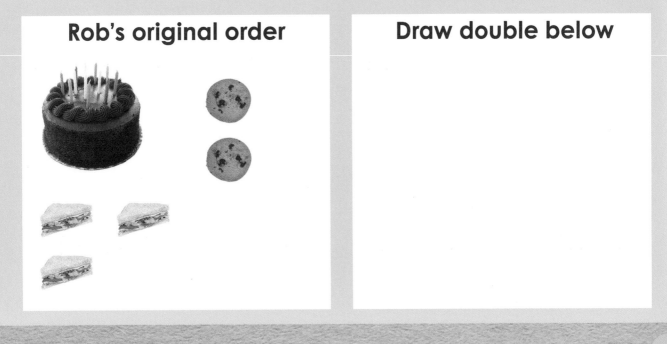

Finding doubles

Spot the **doubles** to help you solve each number sentence.

A double means two numbers that are the same.

1 Find each number's matching pair and write them as a number sentence. The first one has been done for you.

~~2~~ 6 4 7 ~~2~~ 6 3 5 4 3 7 5

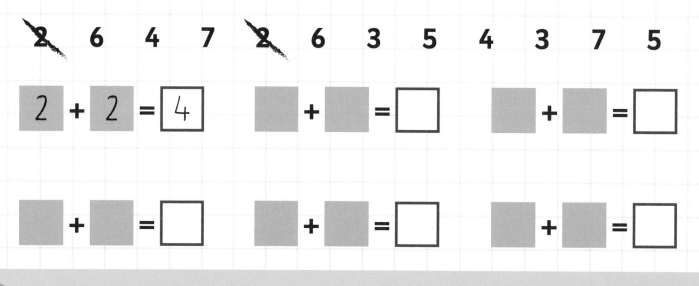

2 + 2 = 4

☐ + ☐ = ☐   ☐ + ☐ = ☐

☐ + ☐ = ☐   ☐ + ☐ = ☐   ☐ + ☐ = ☐

2 Find the pairs in each number sentence and add them together, then add the number that is left.

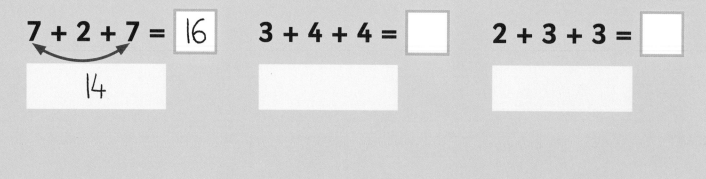

7 + 2 + 7 = 16
        14

3 + 4 + 4 = ☐

2 + 3 + 3 = ☐

2 + 2 + 5 = ☐

1 + 9 + 1 = ☐

7 + 5 + 5 = ☐

Fishing for 5

I know that **3 + 2 = 5**.

When adding 3 amounts together, you need to decide which numbers to add together first.

You might spot an **addition fact** you already know. Try solving that part first, then add the number that is left to find the total.

1. Use your addition to 5 knowledge to solve each problem. Find two fish that = 5. The first one has been done for you.

5   5   5

0   5   1
2   3   4

2. Find a way to make 5, then add what is left over.

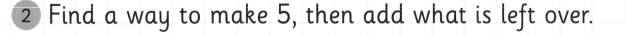

3 + 4 + 2 = ☐

5 + 0 + 3 = ☐

1 + 2 + 4 = ☐

Good guess

Sometimes we don't need to count small groups; we can take a **guess** at how many are there by looking.

1 Draw an oval around the sets with 2 in them.
Draw a rectangle around the groups with 5 in them.

Guessing is also called **estimating**.

How many groups of **2** are there? ....

How many groups of **5** are there? ....

2 Take a look at each number sentence.
See if you have a good idea of how many objects are in each sum before figuring it out. Circle **true** or **false**.

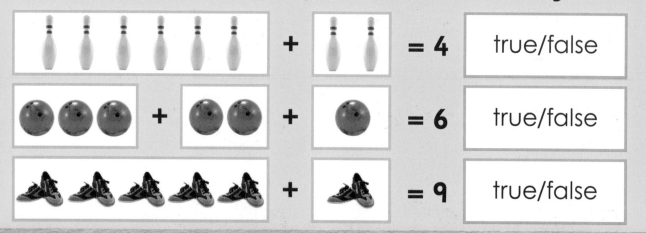

🎳🎳🎳🎳🎳 + 🎳🎳 = 4	true/false
⚫⚫⚫ + ⚫⚫ + ⚫ = 6	true/false
👟👟👟👟👟 + 👟 = 9	true/false

Switcheroo

1 Fill in the missing numbers.

| 2 + 8 = 10 | is the same as | 8 + ... = 10 |

| 6 + 4 = 10 | is the same as | .... + 6 = 10 |

| 7 + ... = 10 | is the same as | 3 + ... = 10 |

2 Organize the numbers into number sentences, then switch them around to write another.

| 5 | ~~6~~ | 5 | ~~1~~ | 10 | 0 |

9	+	1	=	10	=	1	+	9
	+		=	10	=		+	
	+		=	10	=		+	

Solving problems

Use **addition** skills to solve the word problems.

1 In the sports hall, there are 4 basketballs and 3 tennis balls. How many balls are there altogether?

☐ + ☐ = ☐

On the volleyball team there are 2 children with red sneakers and 2 children with green sneakers. How many children are on the team?

☐ + ☐ = ☐

2 Use the drawing space to help you solve the problems.

The children in Ms. Fink's class went to the play park. 6 children went on the swings. 4 children went on the slide. How many children in total were in Ms. Fink's class?

☐ + ☐ = ☐

A group of children took part in sports day. 5 children went home on the bus. 5 rode home on bicycles. How many children took part in sports day?

☐ + ☐ = ☐

Less than and fewer

1 Figure out the **difference** between the amounts below. You can count back in your head to help you.

	is less than		by	
🚜🚜🚜🚜	← is less than →	🚜🚜🚜🚜🚜🚜	by →	2

	is less than		by	
🚜	← is less than →	(9 tractors)	by →	

	is less than		by	
(6 workers)	← is less than →	(8 workers)	by →	

2 Draw in the boxes to show the fewer amount of items.

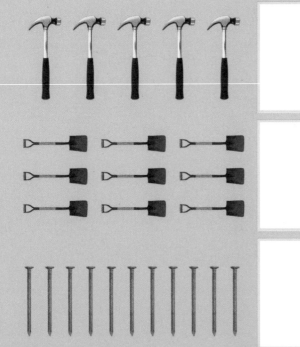

Draw 3 fewer hammers.

Draw 5 fewer shovels.

Draw 2 fewer nails.

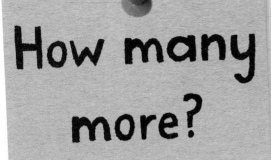

How many more?

Figuring out **how many more** you need helps to solve number problems. Try saying each problem out loud to get used to the words you use when you add or take away.

1 Draw how many more birds are needed on the branch to make 10.

5 + ☐ = 10

6 + ☐ = 10

9 + ☐ = 10

2 Compare the branches. How many more leaves are on the top branch than on the bottom branch?

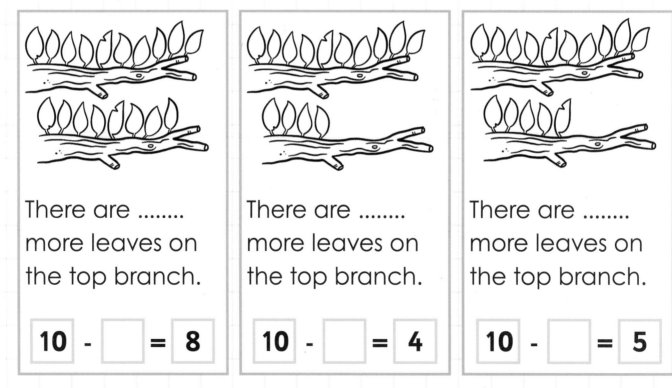

There are .... more leaves on the top branch.

10 - ☐ = 8

There are .... more leaves on the top branch.

10 - ☐ = 4

There are .... more leaves on the top branch.

10 - ☐ = 5

Take some away

1 Cross out the candles to solve the problems.

4 candles were lit.
1 blew out.
How many candles are left burning? ....3....

5 candles were lit.
3 blew out.
How many candles are left burning? ....

7 candles were lit.
4 blew out.
How many candles are left burning? ....

2 Write number sentences to match each problem.
The first one has been started for you.

I had **10** cupcakes. I ate
3. How many cupcakes
are left?

$\boxed{10}$ − $\boxed{3}$ = $\boxed{}$

I had .... cupcakes.
I ate **5**. How many
cupcakes are left?

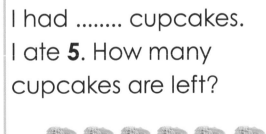

$\boxed{}$ − $\boxed{}$ = $\boxed{}$

33

What do you see?

When we collect **data**, we can organize it in a **graph**. There are lots of different types of graphs.

> Data means information.

1. Use the information from the picture to fill in the graph. Color in one box in the correct column for each creature you count.

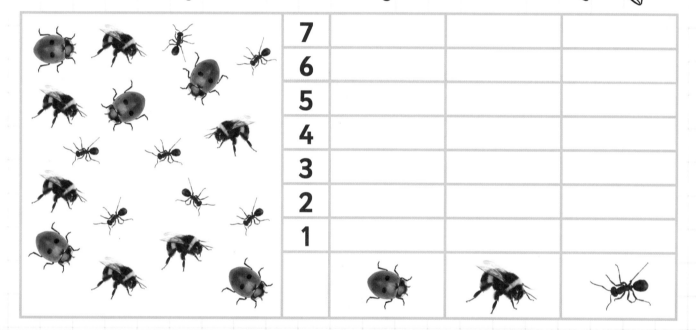

2. Use the graph above to answer the questions below.

1. How many bugs in total are there? ....

2. How many bees and ants are there? ....

3. There are more .... than ladybugs.

4. If all the bees flew away, how many bugs would be left on the log? ....

Flying high

Different types of graphs present data in different ways.

This is called a **bar graph**.

1. Look at the picture and read the graph. Write the correct item total under each bar of the bar graph.

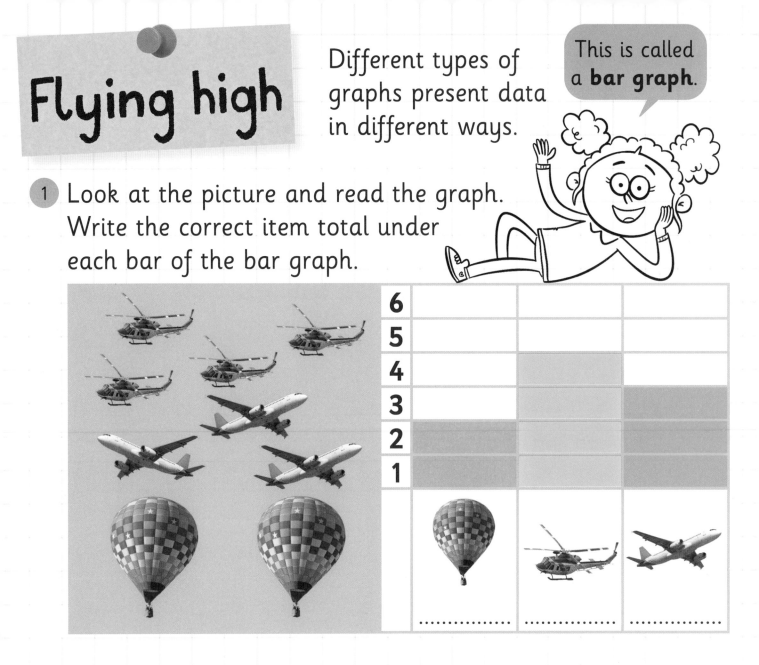

6			
5			
4			
3			
2			
1			
	....	....	....

2. How many balloons of each color can you count? Fill in the bar graph.

6			
5			
4			
3			
2			
1			
	red balloons	blue balloons	yellow balloons

Minus

The **minus sign** - tells us that we are going to take some away.

Subtract, minus, and take away are all words used to describe **-**.

1 Fill in the ten frames as you like, then write **subtraction** number sentences to match.

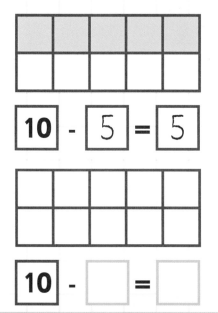

10 - 5 = 5

10 - [ ] = [ ]

10 - [ ] = [ ]

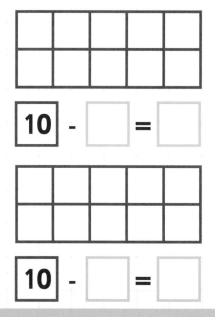

10 - [ ] = [ ]

2 Color the beads to make your own number sentences. Take the amount you color away from the total number.

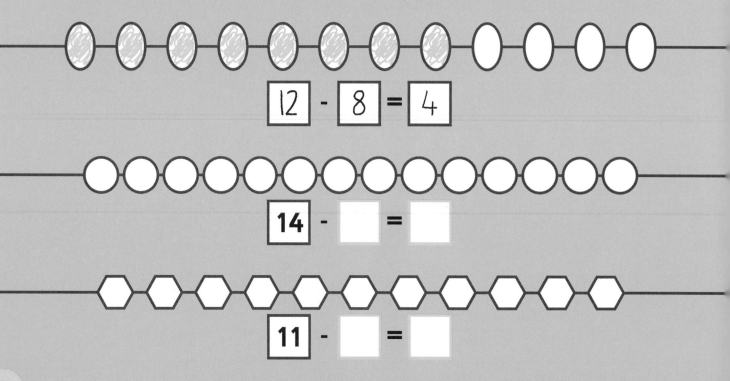

12 - 8 = 4

14 - [ ] = [ ]

11 - [ ] = [ ]

Dino deduction 0 and 2

You can take away by counting back in your head, using your fingers, or using a **number line**.

1 Use the number line to help you figure out the answers.

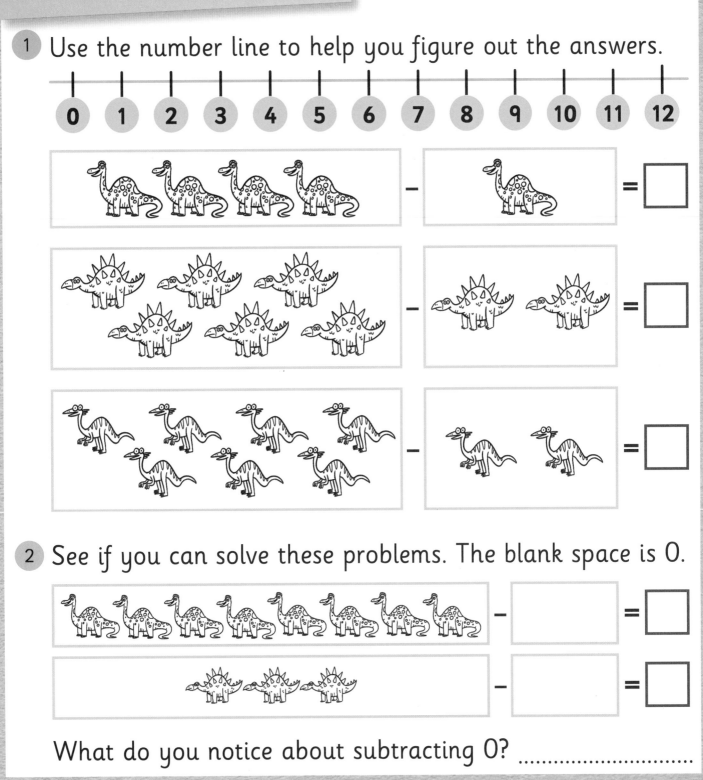

2 See if you can solve these problems. The blank space is 0.

What do you notice about subtracting 0? ....

Missing!

Use your counting skills to find out the **missing numbers**.

Count on to find the number that comes next.

Count back to find the number that comes before.

Count on or back to find the number missing from in between!

1 What number comes next?

4, 5, ...   8, 9, ...   10, 11, ...

16, 17, ...   17, 18, ...   13, 14, ...

2 What number is missing?

6, ..., 8   1, ..., 3   14, ..., 16

18, ..., 20   11, ..., 13   9, ..., 11

3 What number comes before?

..........., 2, 3   ...., 8, 9   ...., 9, 10

..........., 16, 17   ...., 12, 13   ...., 20, 21

Ten frames

Ten frames help us to recognize 10 right away. We don't even have to think about it! We know that a full ten frame = 10.

1 Fill in the ten frames with the correct amount. Write your answer.

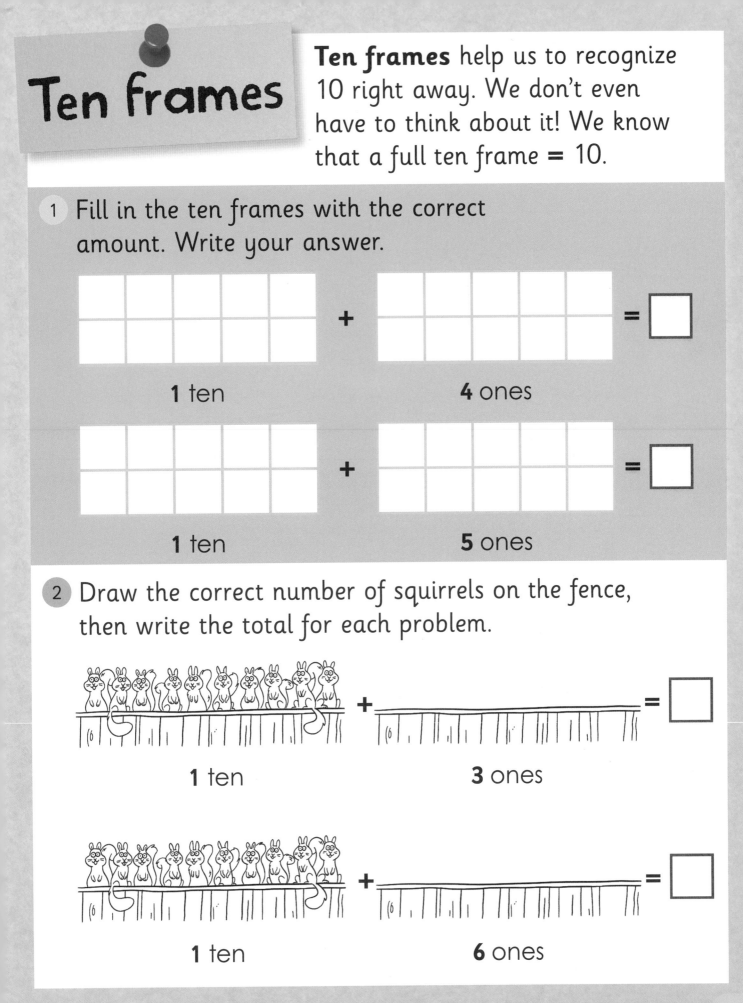

1 ten + **4** ones = ☐

1 ten + **5** ones = ☐

2 Draw the correct number of squirrels on the fence, then write the total for each problem.

1 ten + **3** ones = ☐

1 ten + **6** ones = ☐

10s and 1s to 19

1 Count the **tens** and **ones** to find the total amount of beads.

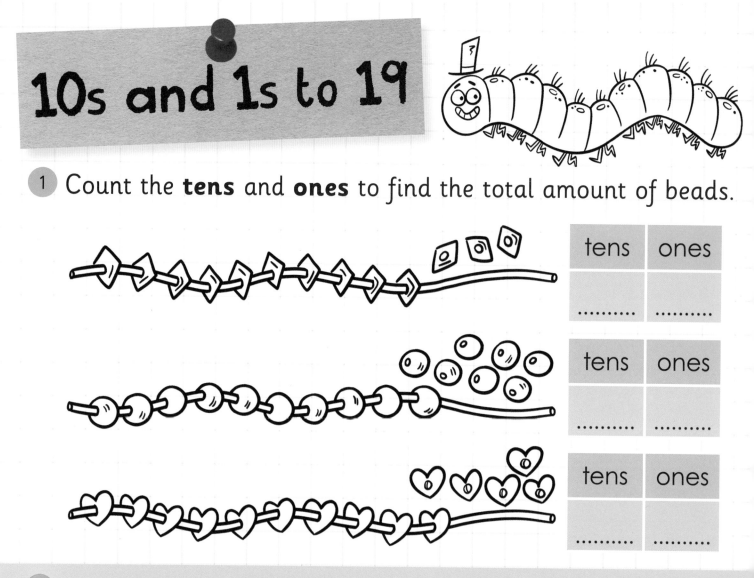

tens	ones
………	………

tens	ones
………	………

tens	ones
………	………

2 Circle the groups of ten and count how many ones are left over.

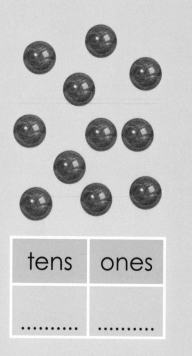

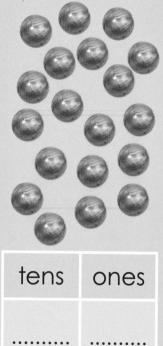

tens	ones
………	………

tens	ones
………	………

tens	ones
………	………

Teens are tens and ones

We know that **teen numbers** can be broken down into 1 ten and some ones.

1 Fill in the missing ones to write each teen number sentence. Color the correct number of boxes and write the number in the equation.

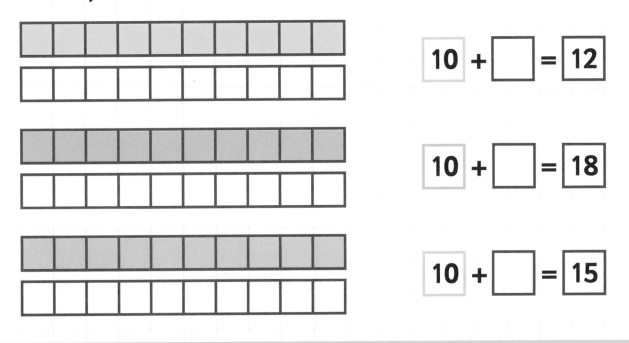

$10 + \boxed{} = \boxed{12}$

$10 + \boxed{} = \boxed{18}$

$10 + \boxed{} = \boxed{15}$

2 Use two colors to fill in the correct number of boxes. A full bar of 10 colored boxes represents one 10.

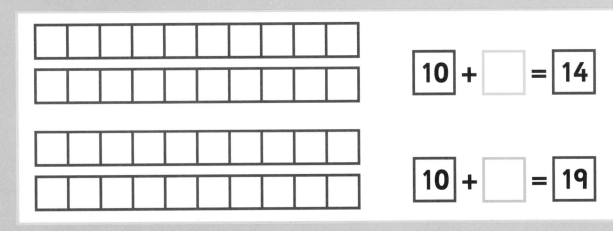

$10 + \boxed{} = \boxed{14}$

$10 + \boxed{} = \boxed{19}$

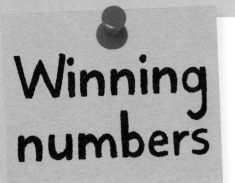

Winning numbers

Teen numbers break down into tens and some ones. We can break down single-digit numbers, too.

1 Find out how many tens and how many ones each number is made of.

11
.10. .... ..1. ....

13
....

10
....

2 Break down each big number to find out how many tens and how many ones it is made of. You can also break down the smaller numbers, too.

15
10   5
5   5   ☐   ☐

16
☐   ☐
☐ ☐ ☐

17
☐   ☐
☐ ☐ ☐ ☐

Comparing length

We can use words to compare different lengths, such as **longer** or **shorter**.

1 Color the longer object red and the shorter object yellow in each pair.

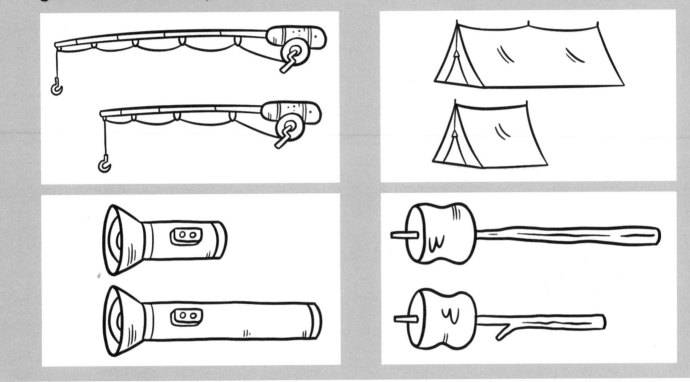

2 Look at the pictures of the children to help you answer the following questions.

| Eric | Jo | Andy | Bill | Amy |

a. Who is the tallest? ....

b. Who is the shortest? ....

c. Andy is taller than
....

d. Amy is shorter than
....

Length investigation

Being able to compare the **length** of things helps us to make sense of the size of things in the world around us.

1 Sort each bar from long to longest and short to shortest. The first one has been started for you.

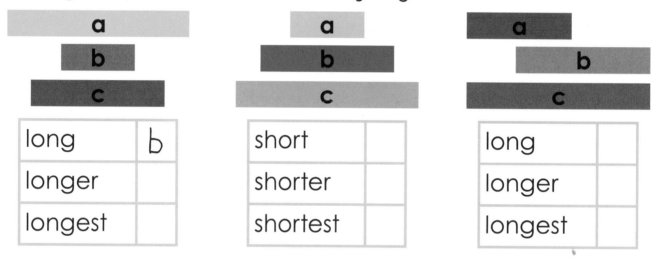

long	b
longer	
longest	

short	
shorter	
shortest	

long	
longer	
longest	

2 Sort the objects from long to longest and short to shortest.

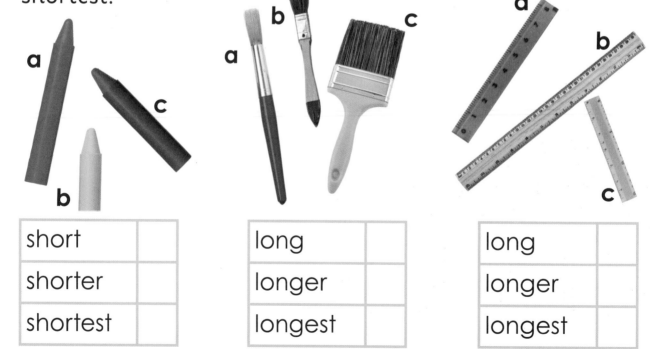

short	
shorter	
shortest	

long	
longer	
longest	

long	
longer	
longest	

Addition and **subtraction** are the opposite of each other. We can change addition sentences to subtraction sentences by switching the order of the numbers.

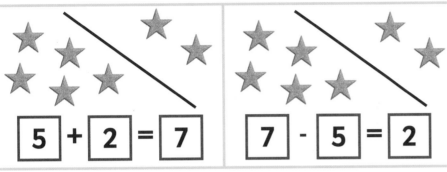

$5 + 2 = 7$ $7 - 5 = 2$

All of the numbers are the same, but they are organized differently for **+** and **−** problems.

The largest number will come first in the subtraction sentences.

1 Write the opposite number sentence for each problem.

$5 + 3 = 8$ $\square + \square = 11$ $7 + \square = 13$

$8 - \square = \square$ $11 - 8 = \square$ $13 - \square = \square$

2 Draw a line between the dots, then write an addition and subtraction sentence to match the problem.

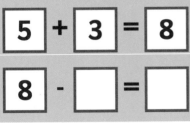

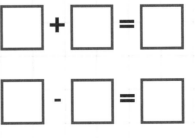

$\square + \square = \square$

$\square - \square = \square$

Build fact family houses

Three numbers make a **fact family**. These numbers can be organized in different ways to create equations.

> Remember! An equation is any type of number sentence with an = in it.

3		7		4
3	+	4	=	7
4	+	3	=	7
7	-	4	=	3
7	-	3	=	4

1. Use only the three numbers in each house to complete the equations in each fact family.

6		4		10
6	+	4	=	10
	+		=	
	-		=	
	-		=	

18		10		8
	+		=	
	+		=	
	-		=	
	-		=	

20		13		7
	+		=	
	+		=	
	-		=	
	-		=	

2. Use your knowledge of fact families to write four equations for the images below.

	+		=	
	+		=	
	-		=	
	-		=	

More monsters

We can figure out what number is missing by using our knowledge of how fact families work.

1 Cross out or add more monsters to solve each problem.

| 5 | + | | = | 8 |

| | + | 10 | = | 15 |

| 15 | − | 3 | = | |

2 Solve the problem below.

18 monsters were hiding in the closet. Some hopped out. Then there were 16 left hiding in the closet. How many hopped out?

There are two ways to solve each problem!

$18 - \boxed{} = 16$

$\boxed{} + 16 = 18$

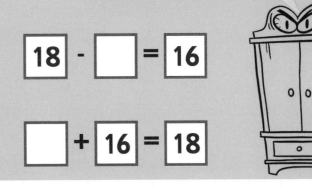

20 to 0

Numbers follow all sorts of patterns. Follow the instructions below and see what patterns you notice.

1 Color in the blocks to match the amounts shown in red and green.

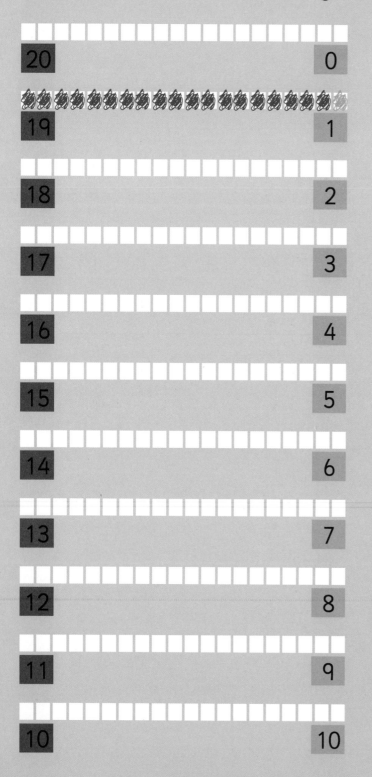

20	0
19	1
18	2
17	3
16	4
15	5
14	6
13	7
12	8
11	9
10	10

2 Use the blocks to solve these problems.

20 - 0 = ☐

20 - 1 = ☐

20 - 2 = ☐

20 - 3 = ☐

20 - 4 = ☐

20 - 5 = ☐

20 - 6 = ☐

20 - 7 = ☐

20 - 8 = ☐

20 - 9 = ☐

20 - 10 = ☐

Racing to 19

Nearly all of the **teen** numbers have teen in their name.

1 Match the numeral, name, and value.

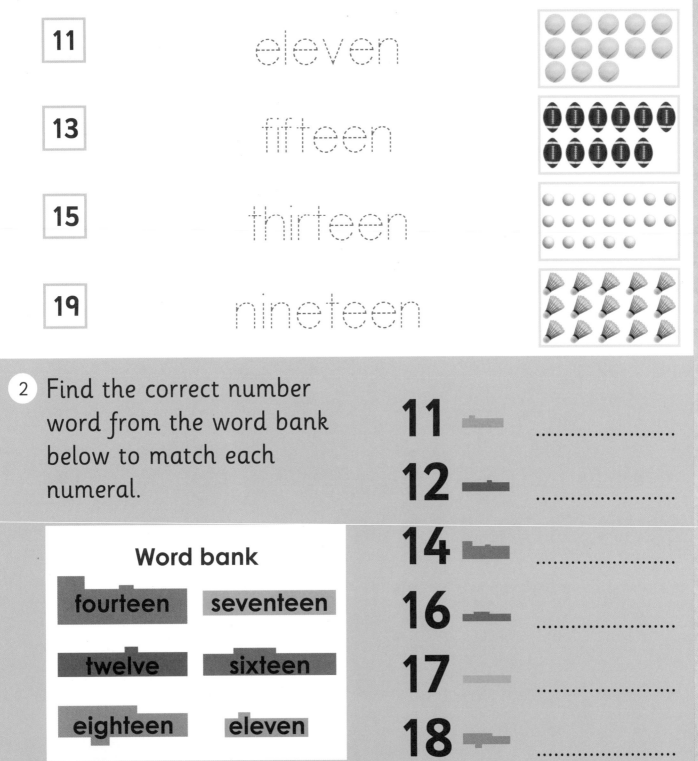

11	eleven
13	fifteen
15	thirteen
19	nineteen

2 Find the correct number word from the word bank below to match each numeral.

11 — ....

12 — ....

14 — ....

16 — ....

17 — ....

18 — ....

Word bank

fourteen   seventeen

twelve   sixteen

eighteen   eleven

Bouncing back

We can **take away** by counting back. When we count back, we jump back along on the number line.

1 Say the target number and count back to find out the missing number.

...... **14**

...... **17**

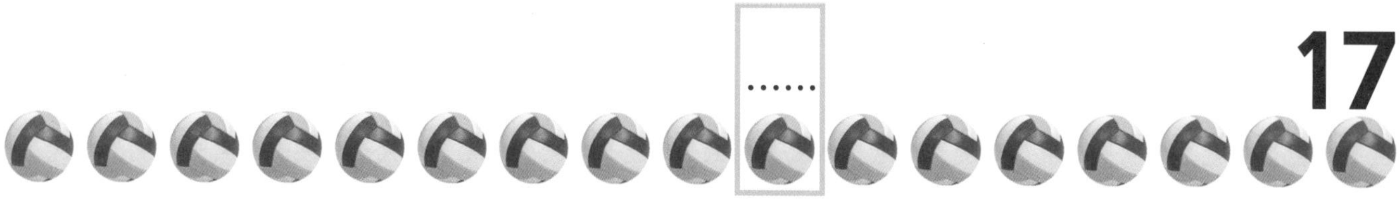

..... **20**

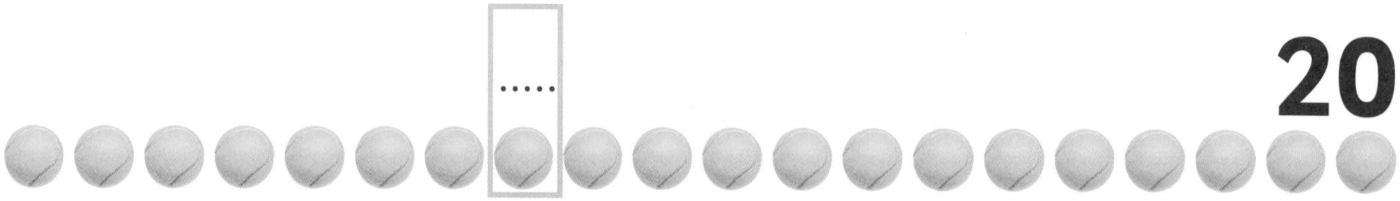

2 Count back to solve each problem.

Cross out the basketballs to help you get to the answer.

$8 - 3 = 5$

$10 - 6 = \boxed{}$

At the fair

1. Todd, Miley, and Adam visited the fairground with their families. Take a look at the pictures of their day and answer the questions.

Todd   Miley   Adam

Who got the tallest box of popcorn? ....

Todd   Miley   Adam

Who has the least people in their family? ....

Todd   Miley   Adam

Who won the most tickets? ....

Who won the least amount of tickets? ....

2. Draw or write your work to find the answer to the word problem.

At the fairground, Adam bought 6 balloons, Miley bought 7, and Todd bought 4. How many did they buy altogether?

Shape shifter

Putting two **shapes** together can create another shape.
See if you can spot any shapes inside this triangle.

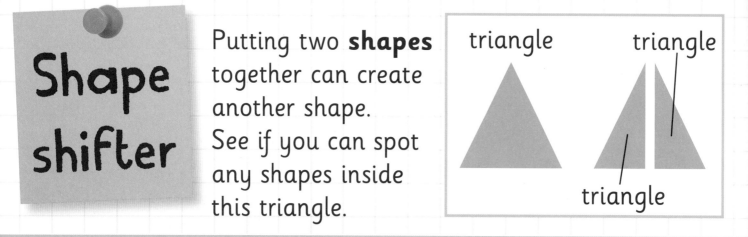

triangle   triangle   triangle

1 Tom dropped the box of shapes and each shape has broken in two. Match the broken pieces to the shape it will make when it is fixed.

2D shape facts

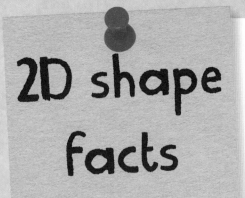

Some things about us change and don't change, too!

Our eye color doesn't change, but how long our hair grows can change.

Defining attributes are things that will always stay the same. For example, a triangle always has 3 sides.

Non-defining attributes can change. For example, a triangle can be big and blue, or small and yellow.

1 Circle the odd one out in each row.

2 Look at the shapes below. Some things will always stay the same and some things will change. Check off the things that stay the same.

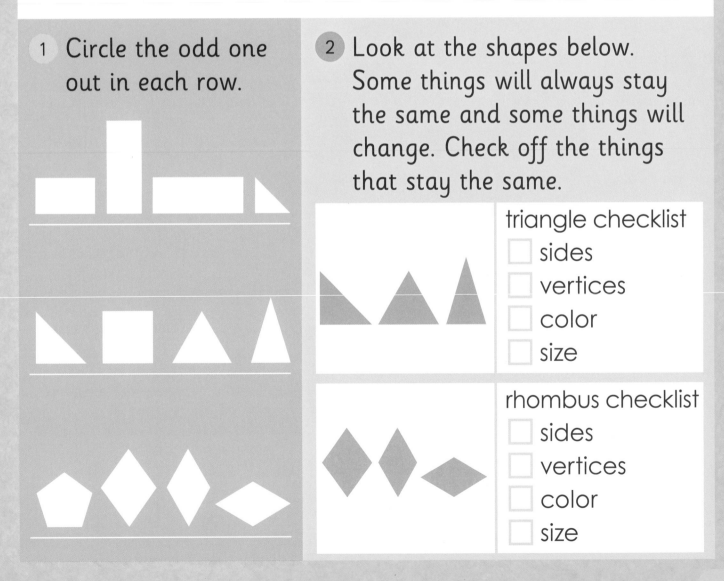

triangle checklist
- ☐ sides
- ☐ vertices
- ☐ color
- ☐ size

rhombus checklist
- ☐ sides
- ☐ vertices
- ☐ color
- ☐ size

Ten frames to 20

Using **ten frames** helps us to create an image in our minds about what equations **= 20** look like.

We show 20 with two ten frames.

1 Use two colors to fill in the ten frames to 20.
Write **addition** number sentences to match.

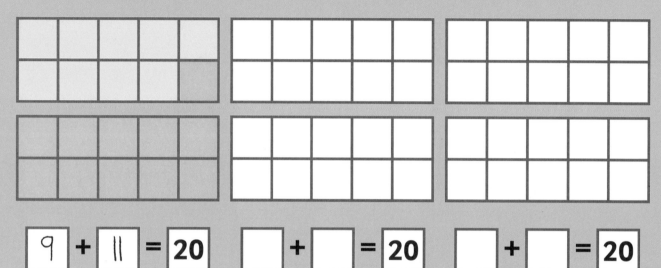

| 9 | + | 11 | = | **20** |

| ☐ | + | ☐ | = | **20** |

| ☐ | + | ☐ | = | **20** |

2 Use two colors to fill in the ten frames to 20.
Write **subtraction** number sentences to match.

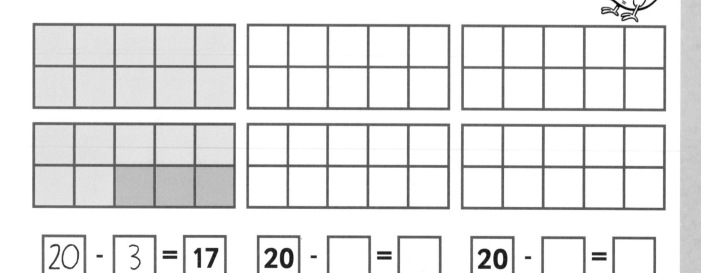

| 20 | - | 3 | = | **17** |

| **20** | - | ☐ | = | ☐ |

| **20** | - | ☐ | = | ☐ |

Tweet to 20

There are many ways of making 20! Let's find some of the ways.

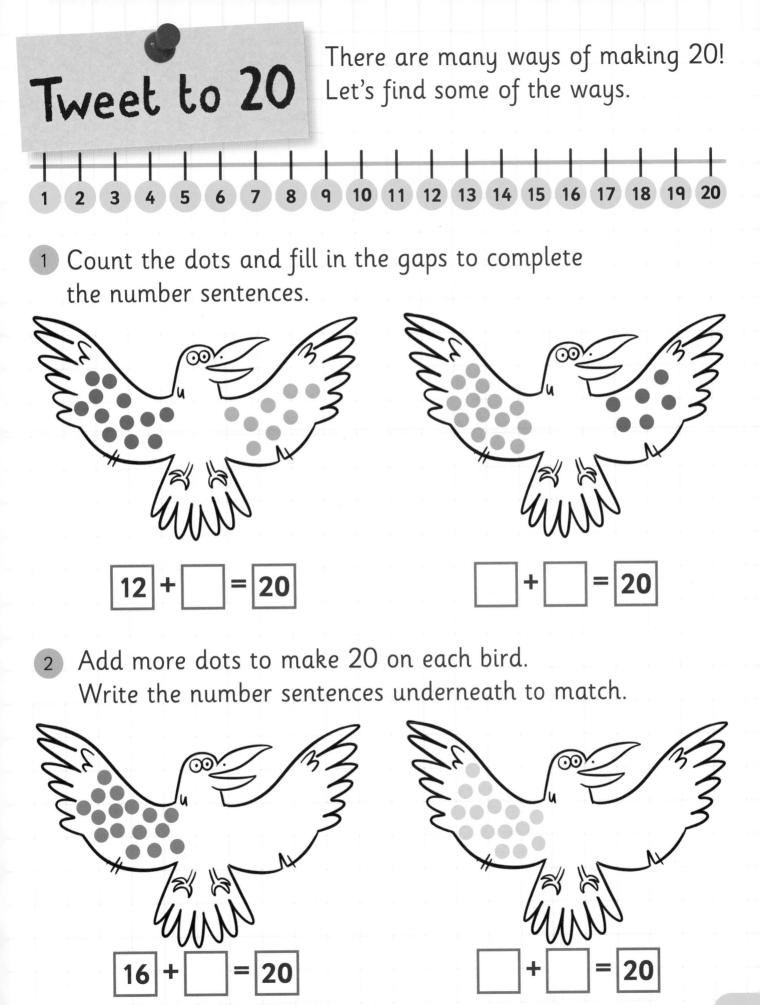

| 1 | 2 | 3 | 4 | 5 | 6 | 7 | 8 | 9 | 10 | 11 | 12 | 13 | 14 | 15 | 16 | 17 | 18 | 19 | 20 |

1 Count the dots and fill in the gaps to complete the number sentences.

12 + ☐ = 20   ☐ + ☐ = 20

2 Add more dots to make 20 on each bird. Write the number sentences underneath to match.

16 + ☐ = 20   ☐ + ☐ = 20

Finding more

As you get more familiar with what numbers and amounts look like, you will sometimes be able to tell which set has more just by looking!

Take a guess first, then double-check by counting which set has more in it.

1 Circle the group that has more in each box.

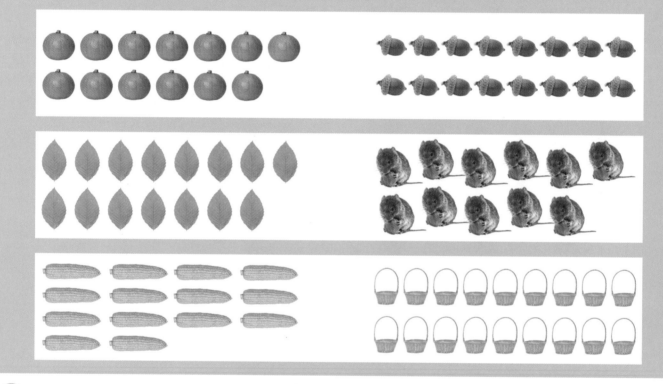

2 Use the pictures above to complete each sentence.

There are 16 ....

There are more pumpkins than ....

There are 4 more .... than mice.

Frog jumps

Put your finger on the starting number and count each jump.

1. Jump along the number square to find the numbers missing from the lily pads.

1	2	3	4	5	6	7	8	9	10
11	12	13	14	15	16	17	18	19	20
21	22	23	24	25	26	27	28	29	30
31	32	33	34	35	36	37	38	39	40
41	42	43	44	45	46	47	48	49	50

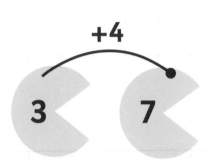

+4

3   7

+9

11

+14

23

+19

31

2. Fill in the gaps in each sentence.

There are .... more frogs than lily pads.

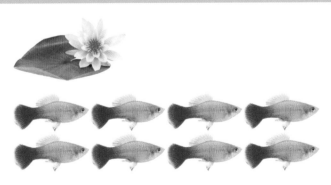

There are .... more fish than lily pads.

57

Gerry's cherries

We use lots of different symbols in math. **>** and **<** tell us about **more** and **less than**.

The part that looks like an open mouth always looks toward the bigger amount!

There are more kiwis than cherries.

1. Gerry likes to eat the biggest amount of cherries he can. Count how many cherries are in the basket, then draw how many cherries should be in the opposite basket to make each problem true.

2. Compare each amount and decide which is **greater than** and **less than**, then add the correct symbol to the box.

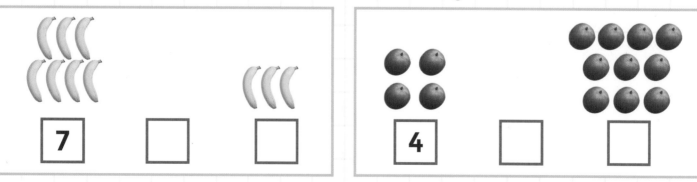

| 7 | | |

| 4 | | |

Adding in order

Organizing the numbers when we are adding can help us to figure them out more easily.

We can add in any order, but if we want to solve by counting on, it can make it easier to order the numbers in each equation from biggest to smallest.

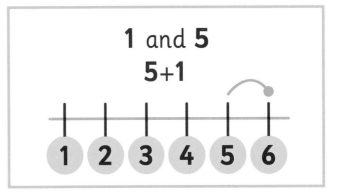

1 and **5**

5+1

1 2 3 4 5 6

---

1 Put the biggest number first and solve each equation.

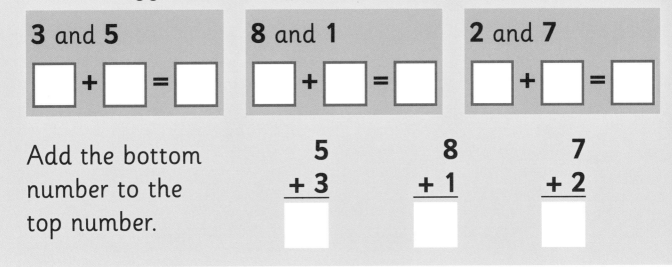

3 and **5**

☐ + ☐ = ☐

8 and **1**

☐ + ☐ = ☐

2 and **7**

☐ + ☐ = ☐

Add the bottom number to the top number.

```
    5         8         7
  + 3       + 1       + 2
  ___       ___       ___
  ☐         ☐         ☐
```

---

2 Count on from 10 in your head to solve each equation.

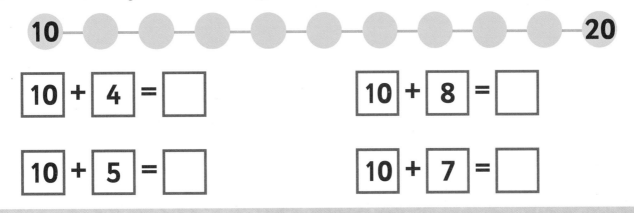

10 ●━●━●━●━●━●━●━●━●━● 20

10 + 4 = ☐   10 + 8 = ☐

10 + 5 = ☐   10 + 7 = ☐

Subtraction in order

In a **subtraction** problem, the number with the greater value must always be first.

| 4 take away **2** = **2** |

1 Put the biggest number first to solve each equation.

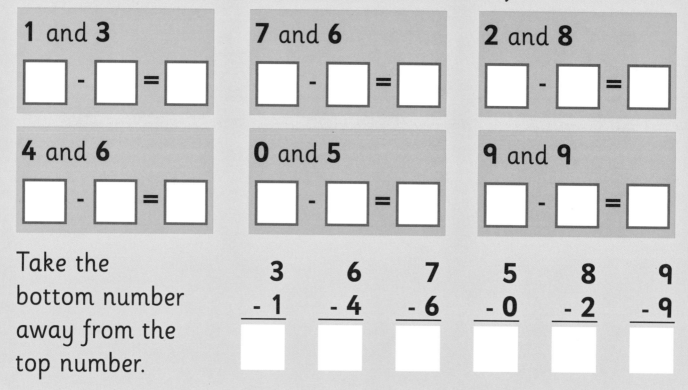

1 and **3**

☐ - ☐ = ☐

7 and **6**

☐ - ☐ = ☐

2 and **8**

☐ - ☐ = ☐

4 and **6**

☐ - ☐ = ☐

0 and **5**

☐ - ☐ = ☐

9 and **9**

☐ - ☐ = ☐

Take the bottom number away from the top number.

$$3 - 1 = \boxed{}$$

$$6 - 4 = \boxed{}$$

$$7 - 6 = \boxed{}$$

$$5 - 0 = \boxed{}$$

$$8 - 2 = \boxed{}$$

$$9 - 9 = \boxed{}$$

2 Count back to figure out what number is missing. Fill in each gap as you figure out what the missing number is.

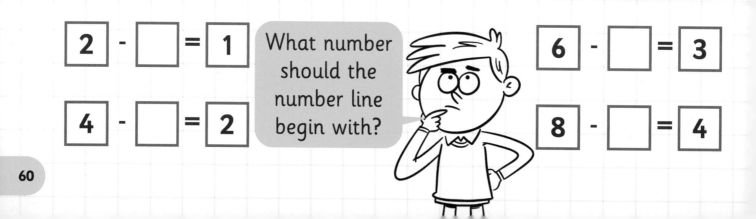

⬤ ⬤ ⬤ ⬤ ⬤ ⬤ ⬤ ⬤ ⬤ — **10**

2 - ☐ = **1**

4 - ☐ = **2**

What number should the number line begin with?

6 - ☐ = **3**

8 - ☐ = **4**

Heavier and lighter

Look at the **balance scale**. **Heavy** things sink down low, and **light** things rise up high.

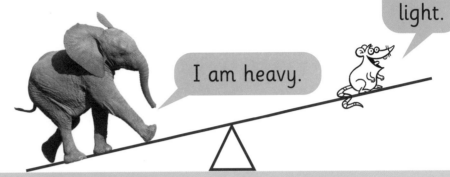

I am heavy.

I am light.

1 Circle the heavier items and cross out the lighter items on each balance scale. Fill in the sentences.

The lion is .... than the parrot.

The lizard is .... than the hippo.

2 To balance the scale, each side must weigh the same. Write the correct number to make it balance.

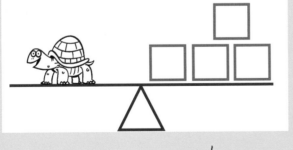

The tortoise and ...4... cubes balance the scale.

The monkey and .... cubes balance the scale.

Balance the scale

Comparing the **weight** of things tells us about how heavy or light an object is. A **balance** is a useful tool that helps us to see which object is heavier or lighter.

1 Draw the correct number of marbles to balance each scale.

pencil	eraser	scissors	glue
2 marbles	3 marbles	5 marbles	3 marbles

The .... are the heaviest.

The .... and the .... weigh the same.

The .... is the lightest.

2 Look at the scales and answer the question below.

A pencil case of crayons weighs the same as ...... marbles.

Sorting odds and evens

When we know the **odd** and **even** numbers up to 10, we can figure out whether a 2-digit number is odd or even.

The second digit in 2-digit numbers tells us whether it is odd or even and follows the same rule as numbers up to 10!

3 is odd   so   **23** is odd

6 is even   so   **36** is even

1 Sort the odd and even numbers.
Write the numbers in the snowballs.

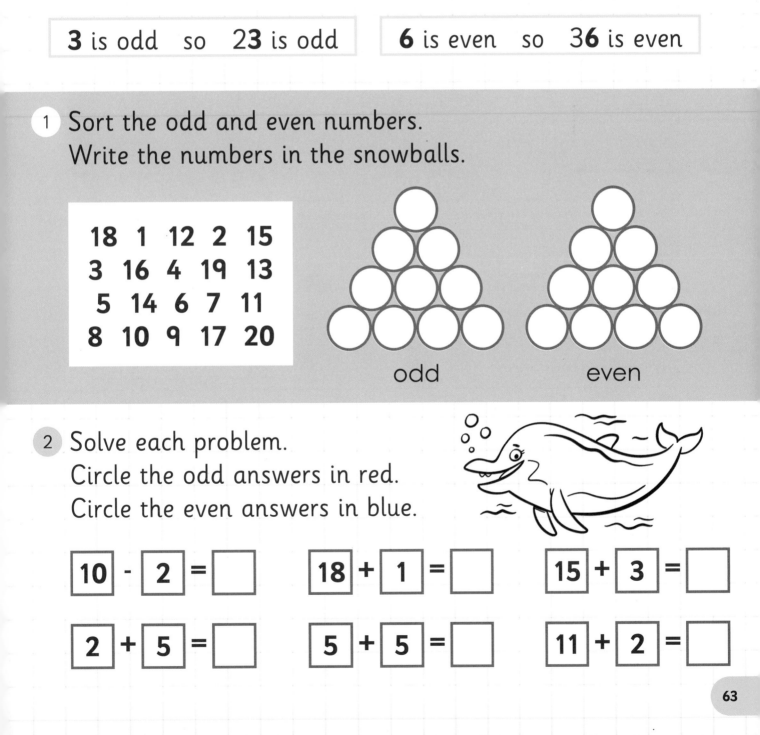

18	1	12	2	15
3	16	4	19	13
5	14	6	7	11
8	10	9	17	20

odd   even

2 Solve each problem.
Circle the odd answers in red.
Circle the even answers in blue.

$10 - 2 = \boxed{}$ $18 + 1 = \boxed{}$ $15 + 3 = \boxed{}$

$2 + 5 = \boxed{}$ $5 + 5 = \boxed{}$ $11 + 2 = \boxed{}$

Build an odd and even wall

① Solve the problem in each brick. When you are finished, circle the answers that are **even** numbers.

5 + 8 = ☐	11 + 3 = ☐	6 + 6 = ☐
4 + 6 = ☐	8 + 7 = ☐	9 + 1 = ☐
13 + 7 = ☐	17 + 2 = ☐	9 + 9 = ☐
9 + 10 = ☐	8 + 8 = ☐	12 + 5 = ☐

② Count in 2s to fill in the missing numbers.

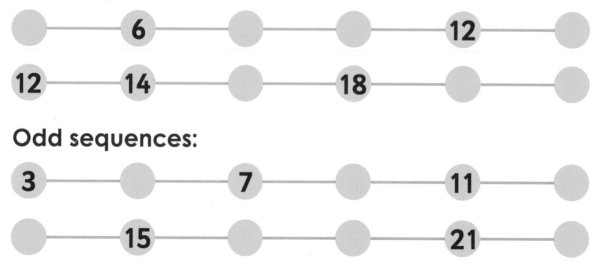

Even sequences:

◯ — 6 — ◯ — ◯ — 12 — ◯

12 — 14 — ◯ — 18 — ◯ — ◯

Odd sequences:

3 — ◯ — 7 — ◯ — 11 — ◯

◯ — 15 — ◯ — ◯ — 21 — ◯

Sharing in half

When we divide something in **half**, we share it into **two** equal parts.

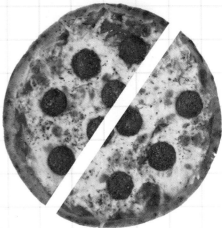

1. Annie and her brother are sharing lunch. Color in Annie's half of the food.

2. ✓ Check the items that have been shared equally.
   ✗ X the items that have not been shared equally.

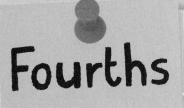

Fourths

Sharing in **fourths**, or quarters, means to share in four equal parts.

Remember, "equal" means "the same."

Another way to write 1 quarter is ¼.

1 All four parts must be equal to be quarters. Color the shapes that are shared in quarters.

2 Draw lines to divide each shape into four equal shares. Color one piece in each shape to show what one quarter looks like.

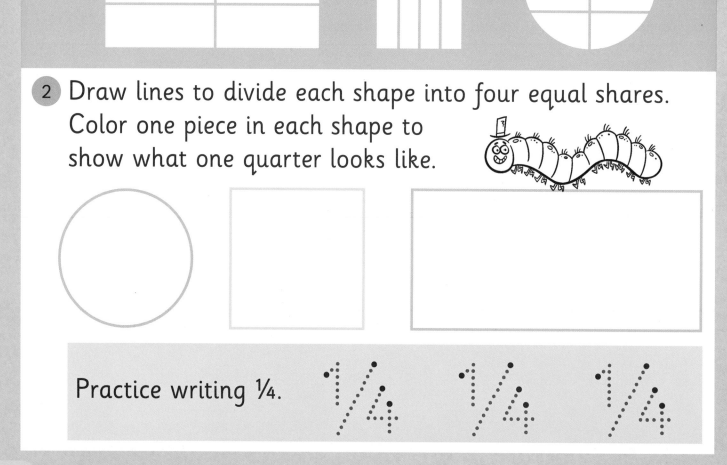

Practice writing ¼.   ¼   ¼   ¼

Halves and fourths

Fourth and **quarter** mean the same thing.

½ = two equal shares

¼ = four equal shares

1 Figure out how many shares each shape is divided into. Color each share a different color.

Label each shape with **fourths** or **halves**.

....

....

....

2 How much of each shape is not shaded? Write ¼ or ½ below each shape.

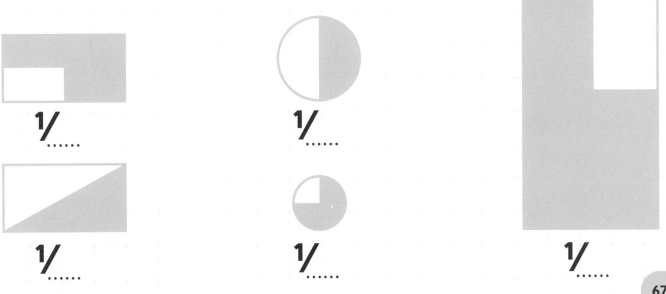

¹/......

¹/......

¹/......

¹/......

¹/......

¹/......

Counting on to 100

Can you count in 1s from 50 to 100? Use the number square below to help, and say each number aloud.

1 Fill in the missing numbers on the number square.

						50
51	52	54	56	58	60
61	63			68	
71			76	79	
	82	84		88	90
	93	95			

2 Write the numbers that come before and after the numbers shown below.

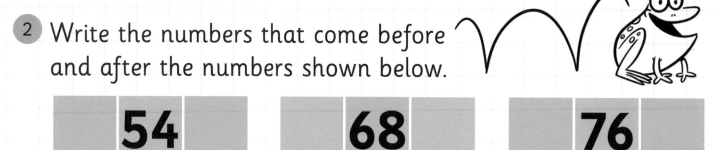

	54	
	68	
	76	

	84	
	90	
	95	

Chocolate chips

There are different ways to keep track when you are counting.

Cross out as you count

Circle smaller groups

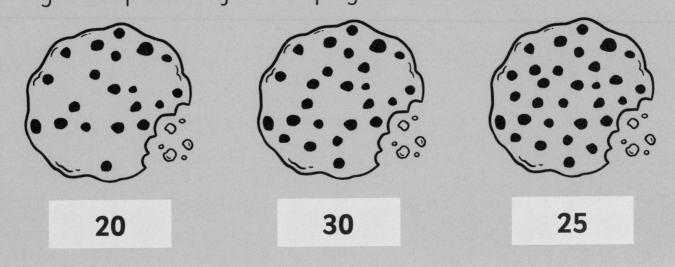

1 Draw a line to match each cookie to the correct amount of chocolate chips. You can circle each group of 5 to help you keep track of the chips you have counted.

20   **30**   **25**

2 Draw the correct number of chocolate chips on each cookie.

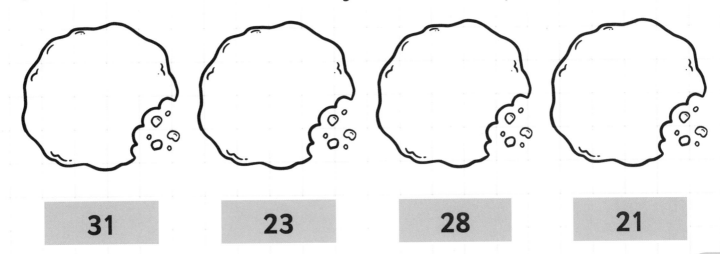

31   **23**   **28**   **21**

Counting in 2s

Counting in 2s means counting every other number. When we count in 2s, we only count the even numbers.

1 Count in jumps of 2 to fill in the gaps.

2	4		8		12		16	18	
22		28		34		38	
	44		50				

2 Count in 2s to find out how many marshmallows are in each cup.

Draw a circle around each pair as you count them so you don't count any marshmallows more than once!

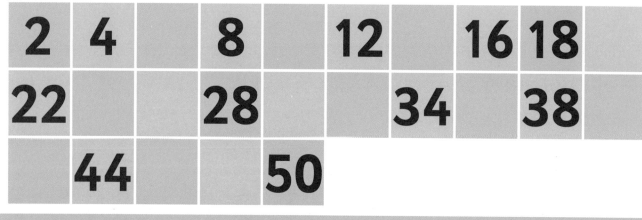

Pirate measures

We can use cubes to help us **measure**.

1 Count how many cubes long each item is.
Write your answers in the boxes below.

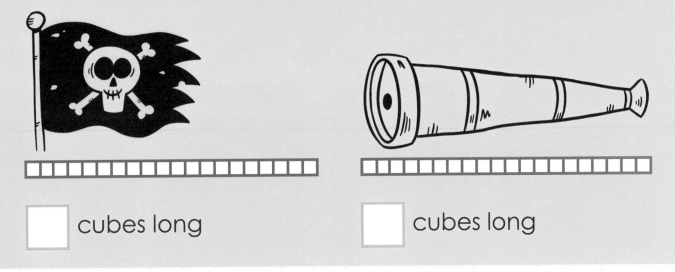

[   ] cubes long   [   ] cubes long

2 When we measure, it is important to be accurate. Count how many cubes long each of the following items are:

sail	[ ] cubes long
flag	[ ] cubes long
boat	[ ] cubes long

Finger or foot

Measure shorter things using your fingertip and longer things using your foot.

We choose what to measure with based on the size of the object we are measuring.

1 Find each of these items and measure how long they are using your fingertip.

Item: **pencil**	Item: **book**	Item: **shoe**	Item: **spoon**
Measures:	Measures:	Measures:	Measures: ....

2 Use your foot to measure things that are much longer than your fingertip, like the length of your bed.

Write the item name.

Measure it using your foot.

Item: bed	Item:	Item: ....
Measures:	Measures:	Measures: ....

Counting in 10s

Counting in 10s is useful when counting bigger sets of objects. What do you notice about the numbers running down the right column?

1	2	3	4	5	6	7	8	9	10
11	12	13	14	15	16	17	18	19	20
21	22	23	24	25	26	27	28	29	30
31	32	33	34	35	36	37	38	39	40
41	42	43	44	45	46	47	48	49	50
51	52	53	54	55	56	57	58	59	60
61	62	63	64	65	66	67	68	69	70
71	72	73	74	75	76	77	78	79	80
81	82	83	84	85	86	87	88	89	90
91	92	93	94	95	96	97	98	99	100

1 The houses are numbered in jumps of 10.
Use the 100 square to help you fill in the gaps.

0 10 ☐ ☐ ☐ 50 ☐ 70 ☐ ☐ ☐

2 Count the groups of 10 to figure out the total number.

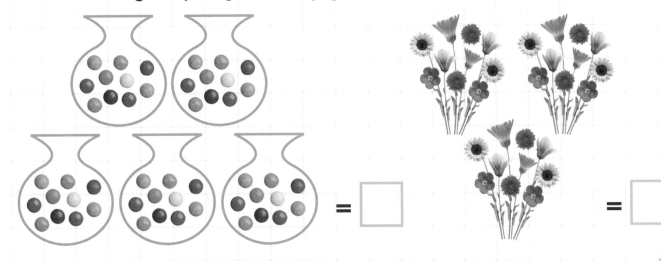

= ☐

= ☐

73

Blocks of 10

Rather than drawing out 10 each time we want to count in tens, we can use a specific picture to represent 10.

— Each block = 10 cubes —

1 Count in 10s to figure out how many blocks there are.

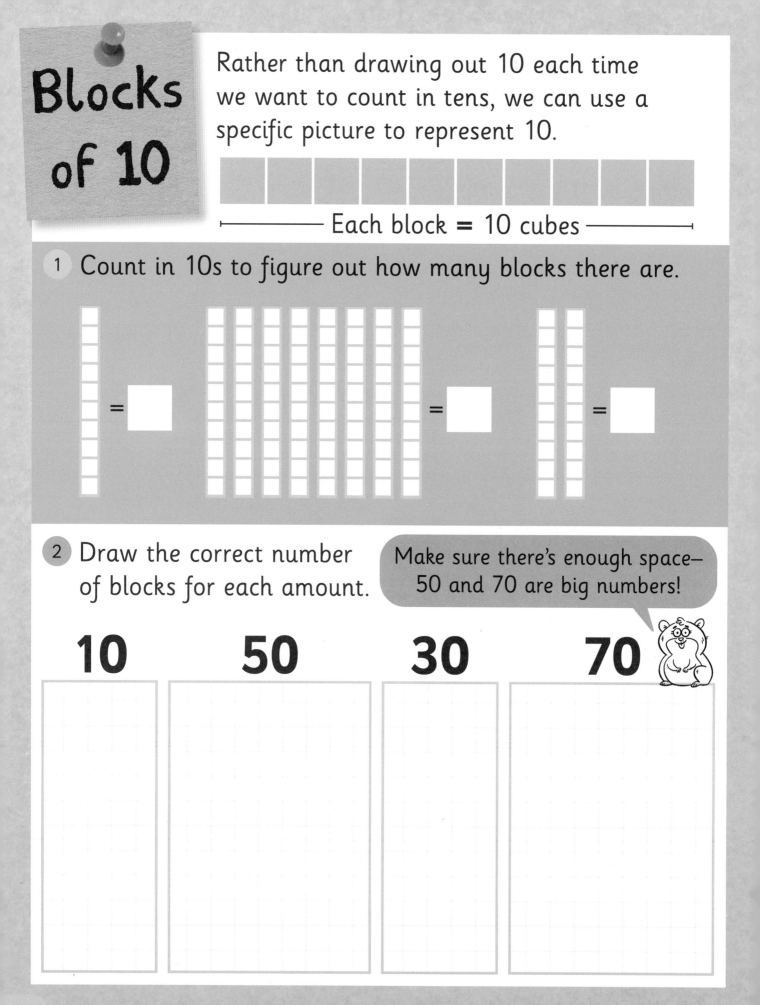

= ☐   = ☐   = ☐

2 Draw the correct number of blocks for each amount.

Make sure there's enough space— 50 and 70 are big numbers!

10   **50**   **30**   **70**

Some 10s, some 1s

Adding bigger numbers can be tricky. Try counting in tens and ones to help you solve these problems.

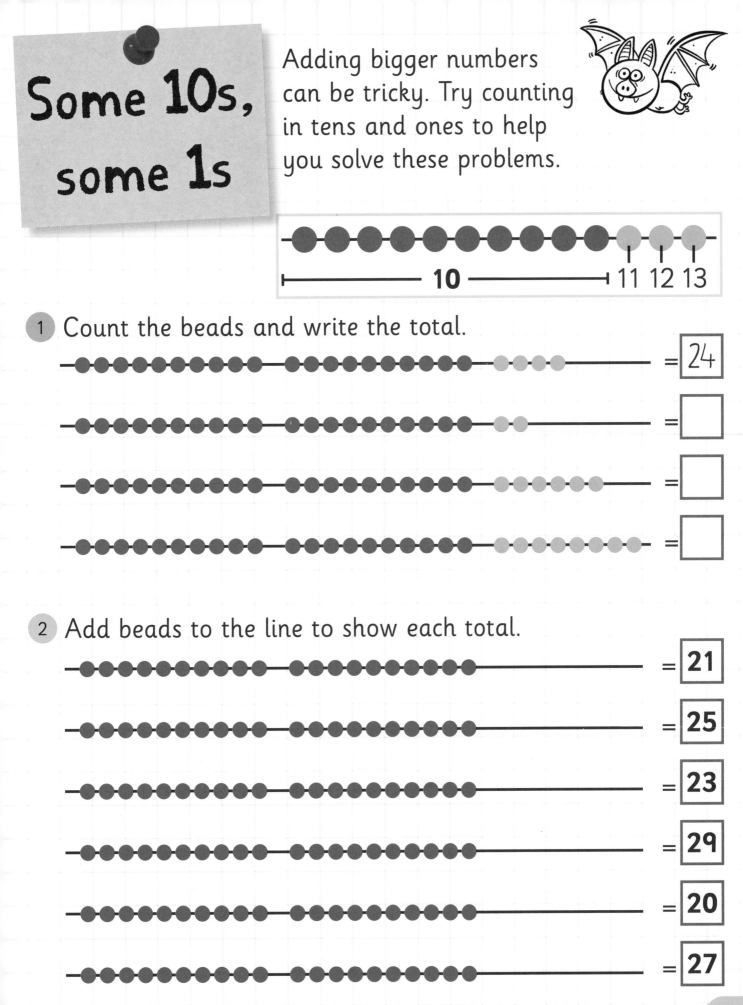

1 Count the beads and write the total.

= 24

=

=

=

2 Add beads to the line to show each total.

= **21**

= **25**

= **23**

= **29**

= **20**

= **27**

Racing forward

Ordinal numbers tell us the position that something is in.

We use ordinal numbers in races, competitions, lists, and many other things in our daily lives.

1
1. Color the first runner's shirt yellow.
2. Draw stripes on the third runner's shirt.
3. Color the fifth runner's shirt orange.
4. Draw polka dots on the fourth runner's shirt.
5. Color the last runner's shirt green.
6. Draw stars on the second runner's shirt.

1st	**2nd**	**3rd**	**4th**	**5th**	**6th**
first	second	third	fourth	fifth	sixth

2 Fill in the gaps with the correct ordinal number.

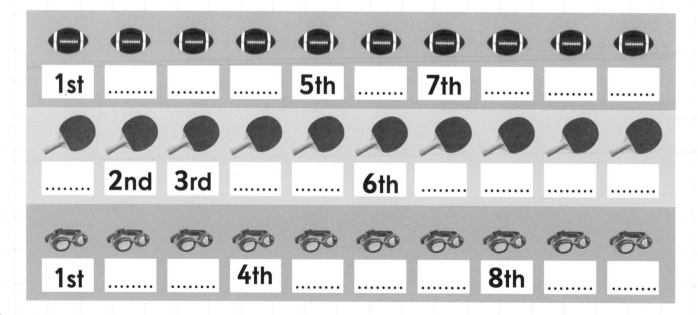

1st .... 5th .... 7th ....

.... 2nd 3rd .... 6th ....

1st .... 4th .... 8th ....

76

Ordinal number challenge

1 Circle the 5th paintbrush.

Circle the 3rd wrench.

Circle the 2nd and 8th hammers.

2 Draw a paintbrush on the 2nd step.

Draw a hammer on the 4th step.

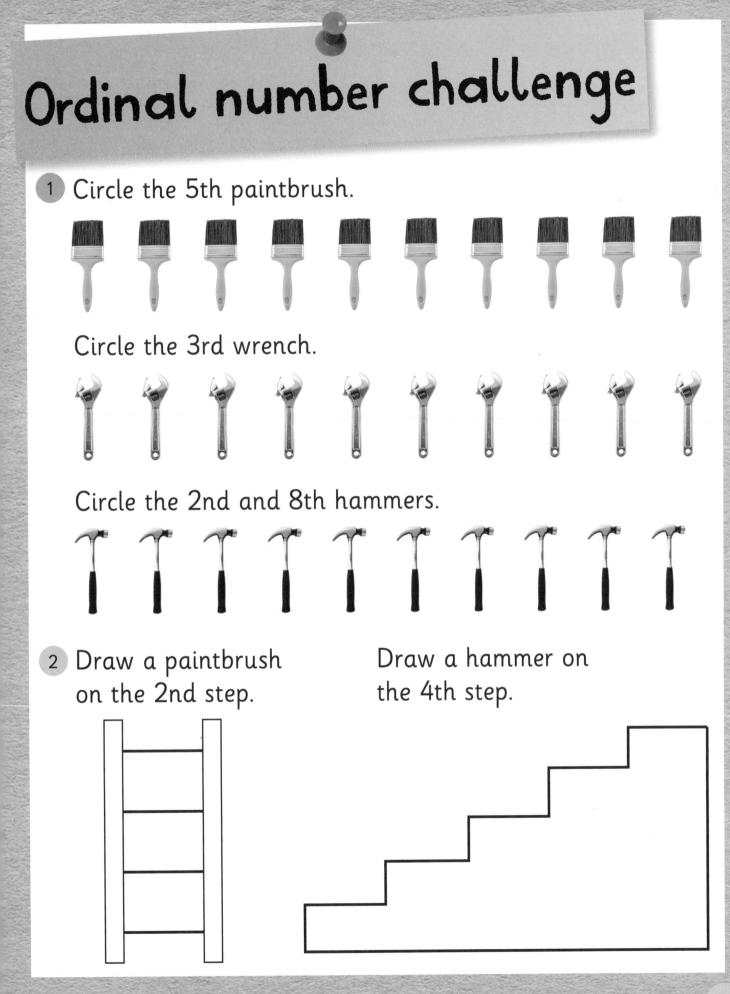

Cauldron counting

Read and say aloud the numbers below.

20 twenty	**30** thirty	**40** forty	**50** fifty

1 Count the items and write the total in the blank spaces.

2 What number comes next?

44 , 45 , ☐   30 , 31 , ☐   42 , 43 , ☐

26 , 27 , ☐   28 , 29 , ☐   17 , 18 , ☐

Bubble gum numbers

Ways to put numbers in order:
- count on
- count back
- sort the numbers by 10s
- find the smallest number
- find the greatest number
- use the 100 square

Greatest means the largest; least means the smallest.

1 Write the numbers from **least** to **greatest**.

23
40 19

32
49 23

19 ....

....

2 Write the numbers from **greatest** to **least**.

24
11
45
33
2

5   13
44
48   30
29

45

High five

Practice **skip counting** in 5s using hands.

High five!

Each hand has 5 fingers and reminds us how many spaces we're moving along the number line each time we jump.

1 Each ogre hand has 5 fingers. Count in 5s to count the total number of fingers in each group.

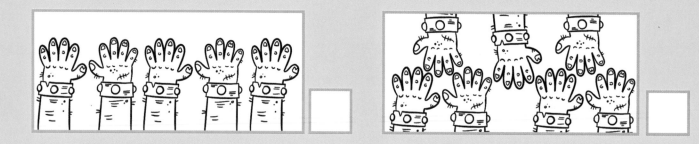

2 How many fingers would you find on 4 hands? Draw the hands and write the total.

Count to 50 puzzle

1 Find all of the numbers from **1** to **50**.
Color in each number only once!

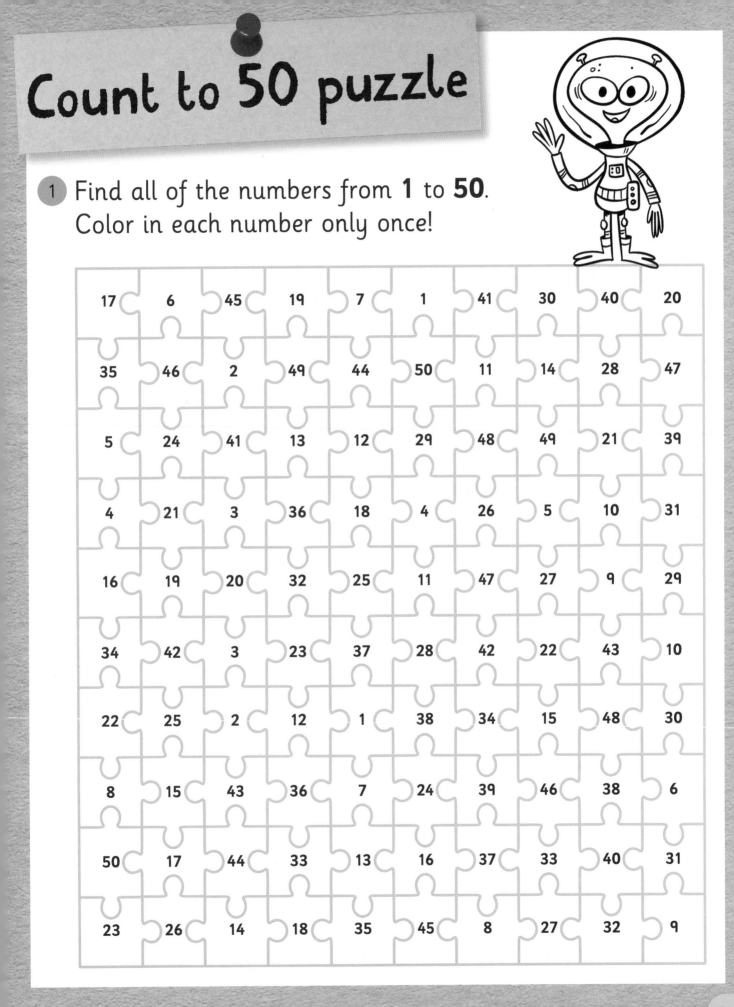

17	6	45	19	7	1	41	30	40	20
35	46	2	49	44	50	11	14	28	47
5	24	41	13	12	29	48	49	21	39
4	21	3	36	18	4	26	5	10	31
16	19	20	32	25	11	47	27	9	29
34	42	3	23	37	28	42	22	43	10
22	25	2	12	1	38	34	15	48	30
8	15	43	36	7	24	39	46	38	6
50	17	44	33	13	16	37	33	40	31
23	26	14	18	35	45	8	27	32	9

10 wizard

When you're a whiz at spotting 10, you can use 10 to solve equations that don't look like they have 10 in them.

Abracadabra!

Find a way of making 10, then solve the rest of the equation.

$$\boxed{9} + \boxed{1} + \boxed{2}$$

$$\boxed{10} + \boxed{2} = \boxed{12}$$

1. Find 2 numbers that add to 10.
Then add the remaining number.

4 + 6 + 2 = ...   8 + 2 + 5 = ...

5 + 5 + 4 = ...   7 + 3 + 1 = ...

2. Sometimes you will need to work a little more magic to find 10. Find a way to make 10.

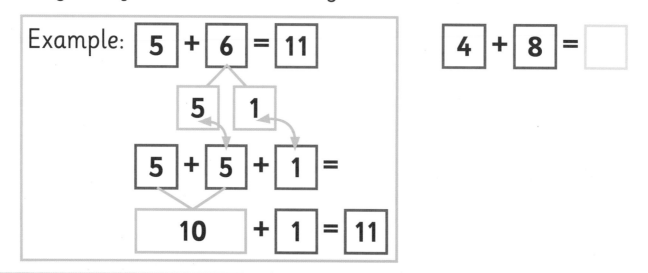

Example: $\boxed{5} + \boxed{6} = \boxed{11}$

$$\boxed{5} \quad \boxed{1}$$

$$\boxed{5} + \boxed{5} + \boxed{1} =$$

$$\boxed{10} + \boxed{1} = \boxed{11}$$

$$\boxed{4} + \boxed{8} = \boxed{}$$

Picking berries

Use your number knowledge of sums to 10 to help you pick the right berries.

1 Pick one number from each bush to solve each problem.

☐ + ☐ + **1** = **11**

☐ + ☐ + **3** = **13**

☐ + ☐ + **5** = **15**

☐ + ☐ + **8** = **18**

2 Now solve these problems.

☐ + ☐ + ☐ = **14**

☐ + ☐ + ☐ = **19**

☐ + ☐ + ☐ = **16**

☐ + ☐ + ☐ = **17**

3D shapes

3D shapes are solid shapes. They have faces, vertices, and edges.

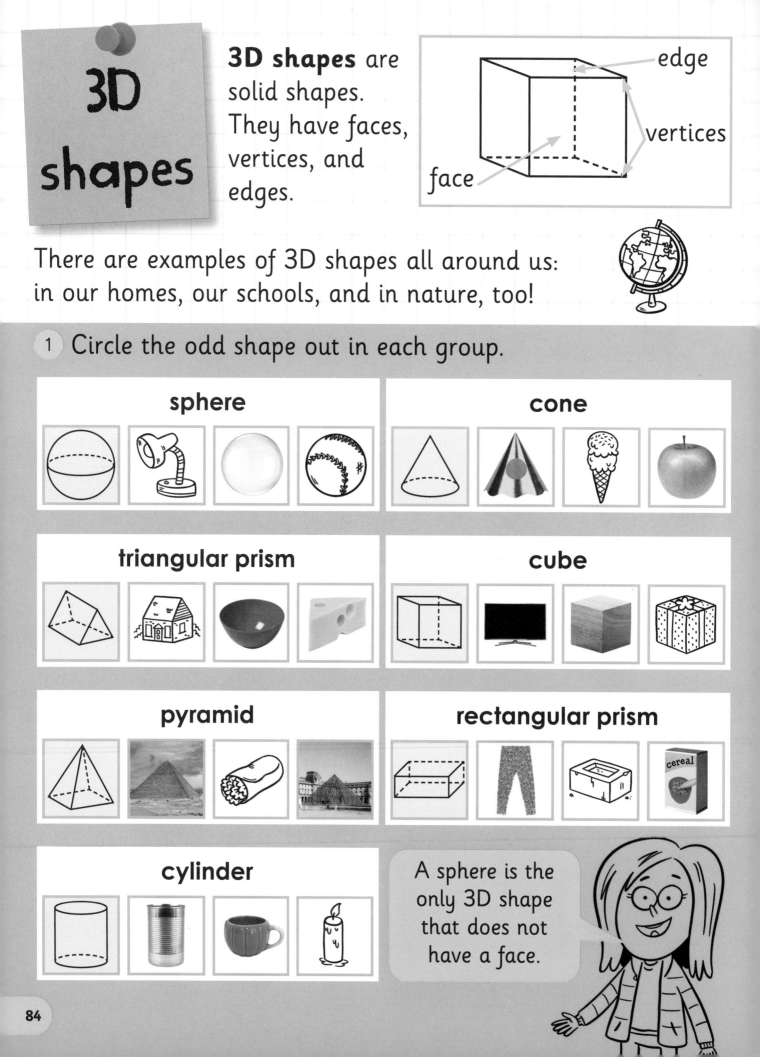

There are examples of 3D shapes all around us: in our homes, our schools, and in nature, too!

1. Circle the odd shape out in each group.

sphere

cone

triangular prism

cube

pyramid

rectangular prism

cylinder

A sphere is the only 3D shape that does not have a face.

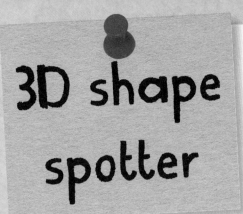

3D shape spotter

We can practice using the names of **3D shapes** by spotting them in action.

Kick a soccer ball? That's a sphere!
Open a can of soup? That's a cylinder!

1 Trace each name and match it to the correct shape.

cylinder

pyramid

cone

cube

rectangular prism

sphere

triangular prism

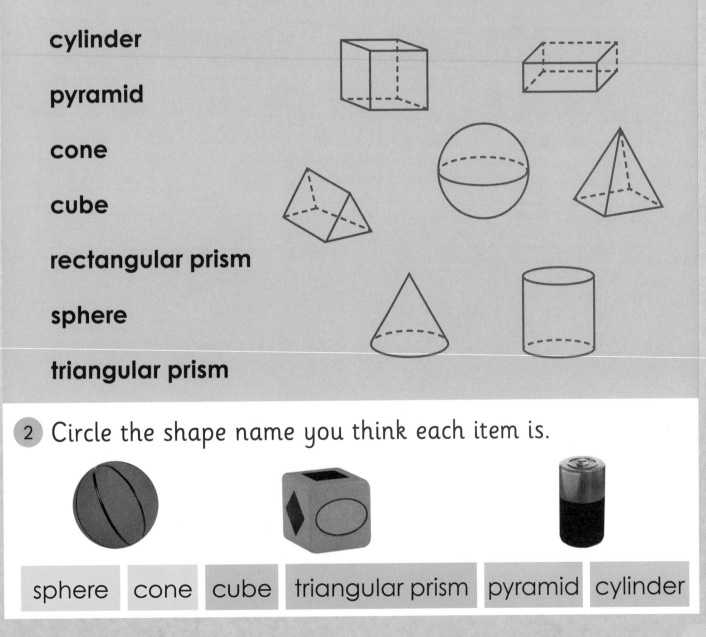

2 Circle the shape name you think each item is.

| sphere | cone | cube | triangular prism | pyramid | cylinder |

Dragon's treasure

1 The dragon's box of treasure is missing some gemstones. Can you draw the correct number of gemstones to make the below statements true?

The dragon should have **28** gemstones in the chest.

There are .... gemstones in the chest.

I need to draw .... more gemstones to make **28** altogether.

The dragon should have **19** gemstones in the chest.

There are .... gemstones in the chest.

I need to draw .... more gemstones to make **19** altogether.

Ladders to 20

1 Fill in the gaps below with the correct numbers or symbols.

20	+	0	=	20
19	+	1		20
18	+	2	=	20
17	+		=	
	+	4		20
15	+	5		
	+	6	=	20
13	+		=	20
	+	8	=	
	+	9		20
10	+		=	

What pattern do you notice in these columns?

2 In each row there is a number sentence that = 20.
Write **+** and **=** to complete the number sentences that = 20.

10		3	+	17	=	20			19
	6		14		20			2	
12			11		9		20		
	1	19			5		15		20
20		0		20		3			

87

Jungle paths to 20

Use this space to draw or write ways to solve the number sentences that you can not solve in your head.

Work it out!

1 Color in green the number problems that add up to 20.

20+0=   10+8=   13-4=   17-1=

15-5=   18+2=   11+9=   10+10=

2 Color in the jungle by shading the leaves that = 20.

7+4   8+8   9+1

13+6   11+9

13+7   10+10   6+14

16+2

20+0   3+5

8+12   5+5   1+15

All aboard the bus

Solving word problems is easier when we create a picture in our minds about what is happening.

At the bus stop.

1 Read the problem, then fill in the answer. Use the picture below to help.

There are **3** free seats on the bus.
5 children want to get on.
How many children will not have a seat? ....

2 Write a subtraction sentence for each picture.

Tick tock

Analog **clocks** have numbers and hands on them. The long hand tells us what minute it is and the short hand tells us what hour we are in.

Analog

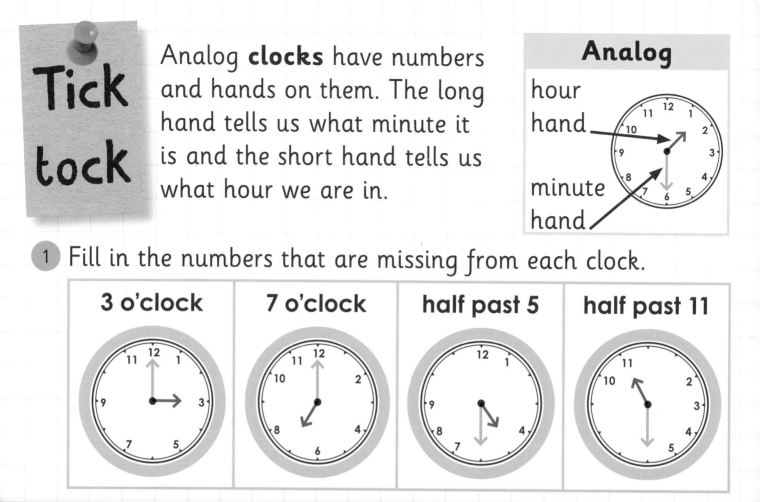

1 Fill in the numbers that are missing from each clock.

| 3 o'clock | 7 o'clock | half past 5 | half past 11 |

2 When the minute hand is at 12, the hour hand will point directly at a number, telling us what hour it is.
Write the time underneath each clock.

3 .... o'clock   .... o'clock   .... o'clock   .... o'clock

Just like this!

.... o'clock   .... o'clock

Half past

There are 60 minutes in an hour.
There are 30 minutes in half an hour.

When the minute hand points to 6, it is telling us that the hand has traveled halfway around the clock. It is 30 minutes after the hour.

At half past, the hour hand is halfway between two hours.

1 The hour hand tells us what hours we are in between. Fill in the gaps to tell the time on each clock.

half past ...l...

half past ....

half past ....

half past ....

2 Add the minute and hour hands to show the new times on the clocks.

- 1 hour	current time	+ 1 hour

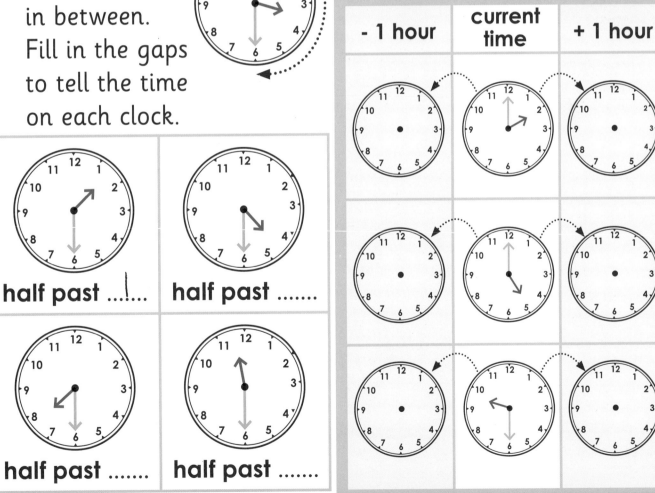

Join the dots from 0 to 120

Starting at...

You know your numbers, but can you count on from any number? Challenge time!

Count to 66. Start at 30.	Count to 99. Start at 70.	Count to 100. Start at 55.

① Fill in the gaps in these monster number lines.

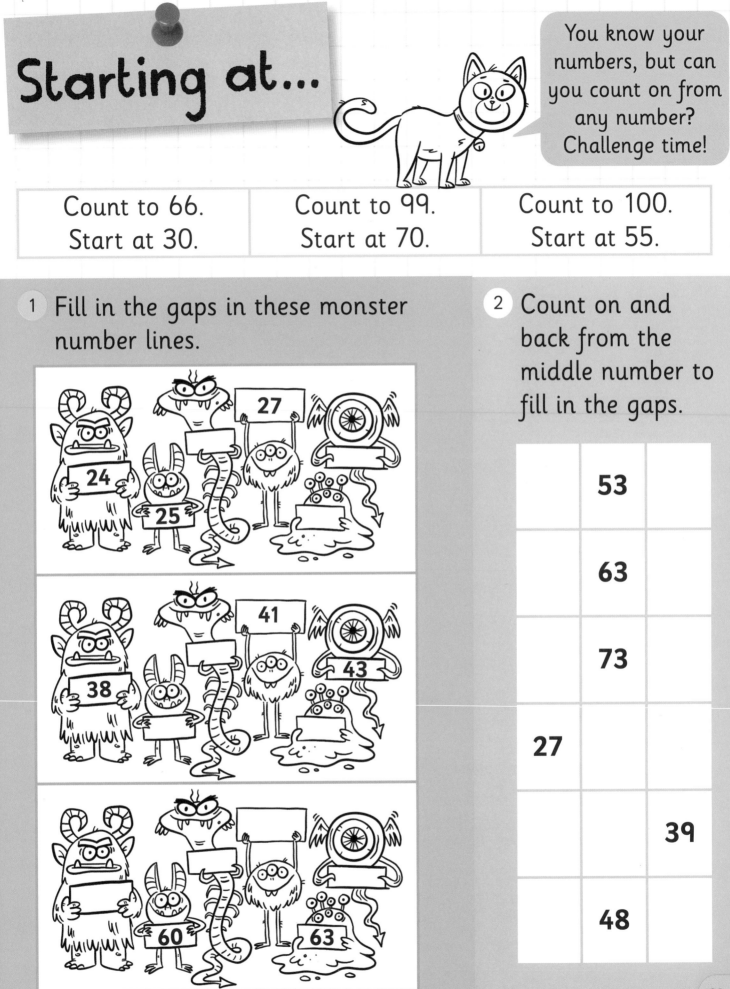

② Count on and back from the middle number to fill in the gaps.

	53	
	63	
	73	
27		
		39
	48	

Taking away tens

1 Cross out the tens to solve each equation.

$$30 - 10 = \boxed{}$$

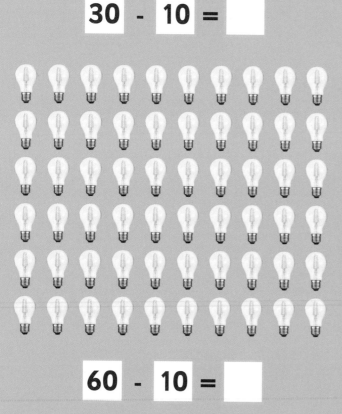

$$60 - 10 = \boxed{}$$

$$10 - 10 = \boxed{}$$

2 Jump back in tens. Finish the subtraction sentences to match each jump.

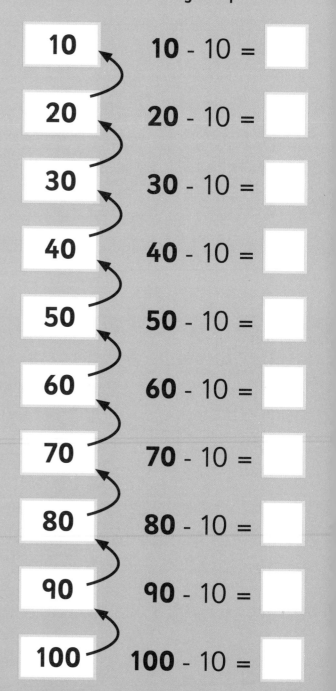

$10 - 10 = \boxed{}$

$20 - 10 = \boxed{}$

$30 - 10 = \boxed{}$

$40 - 10 = \boxed{}$

$50 - 10 = \boxed{}$

$60 - 10 = \boxed{}$

$70 - 10 = \boxed{}$

$80 - 10 = \boxed{}$

$90 - 10 = \boxed{}$

$100 - 10 = \boxed{}$

Tens and ones to 50

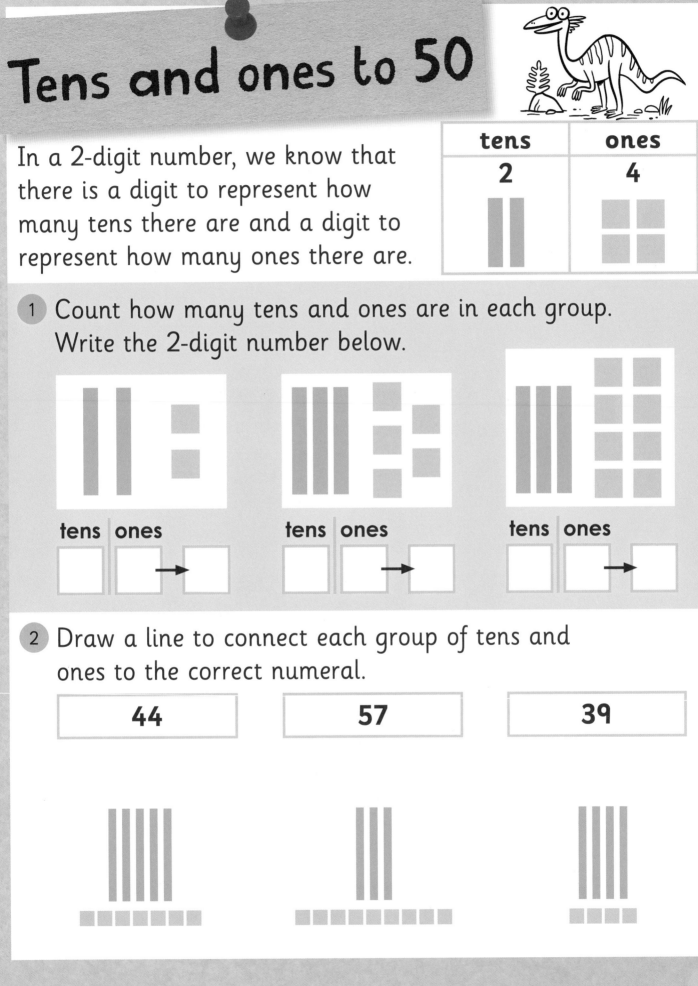

In a 2-digit number, we know that there is a digit to represent how many tens there are and a digit to represent how many ones there are.

tens	ones
2	4

1 Count how many tens and ones are in each group. Write the 2-digit number below.

tens | ones

tens | ones

tens | ones

2 Draw a line to connect each group of tens and ones to the correct numeral.

| 44 | 57 | 39 |

10 more
10 less

When figuring out 10 more or 10 less, we **jump back** or **jump forward** 10 spaces on the 100 square.

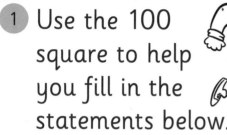

1 Use the 100 square to help you fill in the statements below.

1	2	3	4	5	6	7	8	9	10
11	12	13	14	15	16	17	18	19	20
21	22	23	24	25	26	27	28	29	30
31	32	33	34	35	36	37	38	39	40
41	42	43	44	45	46	47	48	49	50
51	52	53	54	55	56	57	58	59	60
61	62	63	64	65	66	67	68	69	70
71	72	73	74	75	76	77	78	79	80
81	82	83	84	85	86	87	88	89	90
91	92	93	94	95	96	97	98	99	100

.... is 10 more than 12.

.... is 10 less than 85.

56 is 10 more than ....

2 Using the 100 square, find out what is **10 more** and **10 less** in each of these problems.

Liam has 8 toy cars. Sophia has 10 more. How many cars does Sophia have? ....

Eli has 40 yo-yos. Mason has 10 fewer. How many yo-yos does Mason have? ....

Mila has 10 more crayons than Josh. Josh has 23 crayons. How many crayons does Mila have? ....

Louisa has 67 puzzle pieces. Jonas has 10 fewer. How many puzzle pieces does Jonas have? ....

Adding to double digits

When we add 2-digit and 1-digit numbers together, we focus on the tens and ones separately at first.

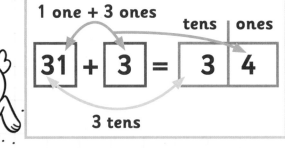

1 one + 3 ones

tens | ones

$31 + 3 = $ | 3 | 4

3 tens

---

1 Add the ones first, then solve each equation.

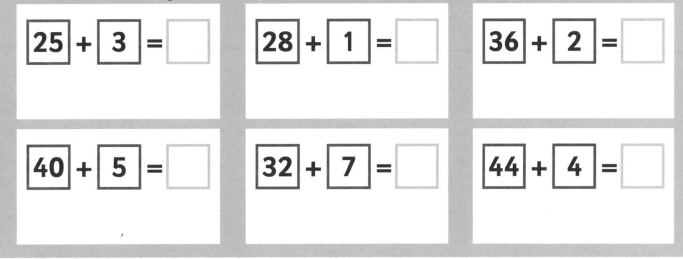

$25 + 3 = \square$

$28 + 1 = \square$

$36 + 2 = \square$

$40 + 5 = \square$

$32 + 7 = \square$

$44 + 4 = \square$

When you add or take away 10, only the tens will change because any number + or - 0 stays the same.

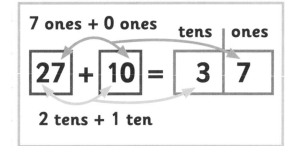

7 ones + 0 ones

tens | ones

$27 + 10 = $ | 3 | 7

2 tens + 1 ten

2 Solve each equation.

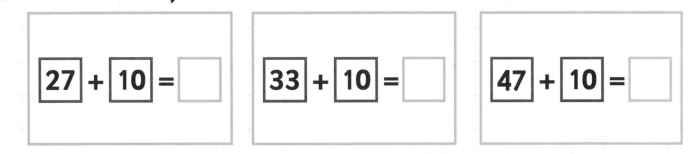

$27 + 10 = \square$

$33 + 10 = \square$

$47 + 10 = \square$

Flower power

There are ten flowers in each bunch.

Now try putting the two skills together.

10   20   1

1. Counting in tens and in ones, find out the value of each group.

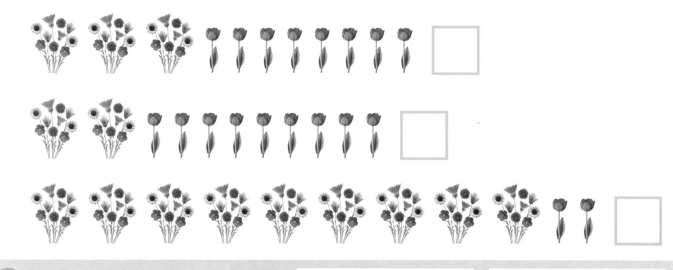

2. Draw a rectangle to represent ten and a thin line to represent one to show the value.

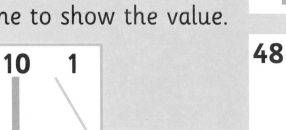

23	52
48	86

Blast-off!

1 Draw a tally for how many of the following items you can find.

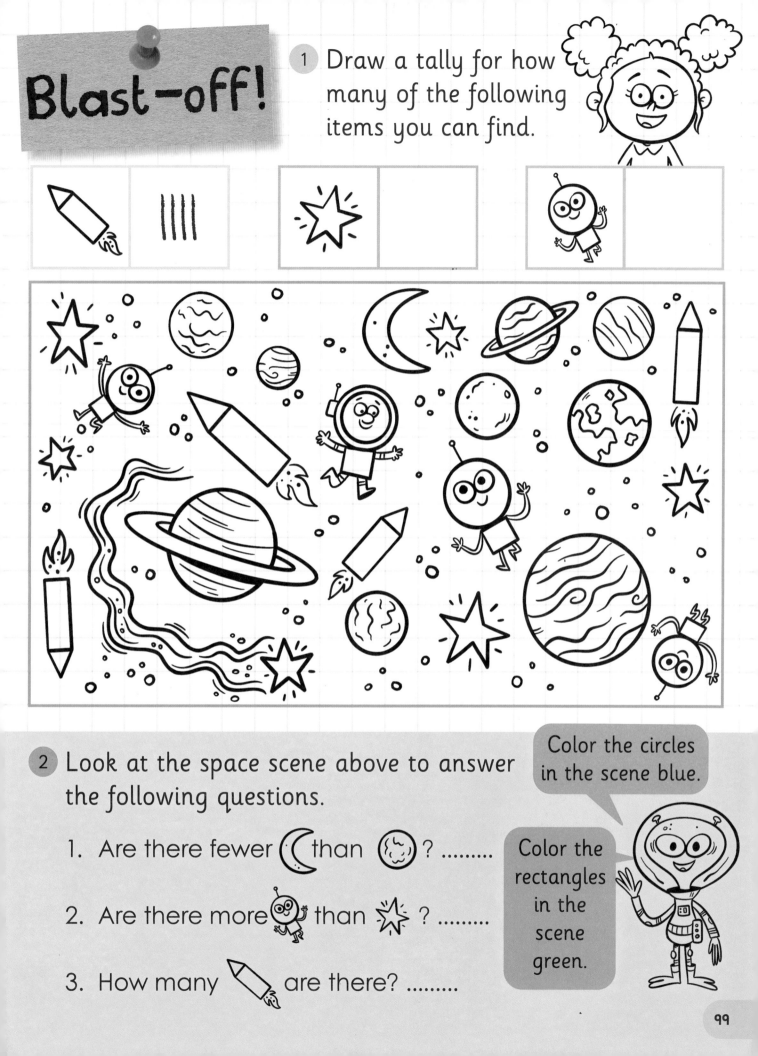

2 Look at the space scene above to answer the following questions.

Color the circles in the scene blue.

1. Are there fewer 🌙 than 🌑? ....

Color the rectangles in the scene green.

2. Are there more 👽 than ✨? ....

3. How many ✏️ are there? ....

Ordering numbers

Order numbers by **counting on** or **counting back**.

If you can count to 100, you can order numbers to 100!

1 Count in ones to fill in the gaps on the flags.

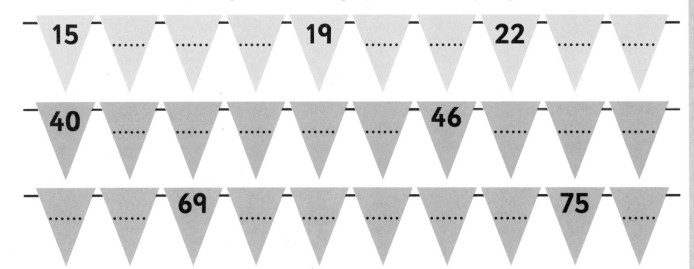

15 .... **19** .... **22** ....

40 .... **46** ....

.... **69** .... **75** ......

2 Count on and back in 2s and 5s to fill the gaps.

-2	
....	**44**
....	**72**
....	**86**

+2	
30	....
58	....
92	....

-5	
....	**65**
....	**80**
....	**45**

+5	
75	....
90	....
30	....

Number line hop to 99

Use your number knowledge to solve each challenge.

1 Begin at 28. Jump forward 2. What number did you land on? ....

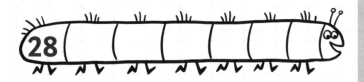

Begin at 47. Jump forward 5. What number did you land on? ....

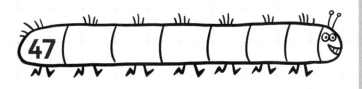

Begin at 80. Jump back 6. What number did you land on? ....

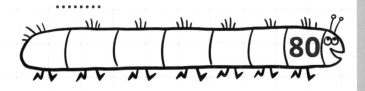

2 Read the clues to figure out the correct number. Use the 100 square to help.

I am 10 less than 69.
I am ....

I have 5 tens and the same number of ones.
I am ....

I am 20 more than 71.
I am ....

I have 7 tens. I have more than 8 ones. I am ....

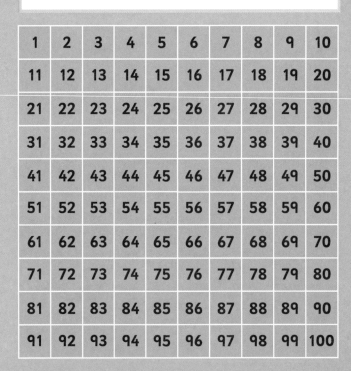

1	2	3	4	5	6	7	8	9	10
11	12	13	14	15	16	17	18	19	20
21	22	23	24	25	26	27	28	29	30
31	32	33	34	35	36	37	38	39	40
41	42	43	44	45	46	47	48	49	50
51	52	53	54	55	56	57	58	59	60
61	62	63	64	65	66	67	68	69	70
71	72	73	74	75	76	77	78	79	80
81	82	83	84	85	86	87	88	89	90
91	92	93	94	95	96	97	98	99	100

Greater than, less than, equal

We use symbols to show when a number or equation is **greater than**, **less than**, or **equal to**.

>	<	=
greater than	**less** than	**equal** to

1 Compare the numbers. Decide which symbol tells you about each pair. < >

14		21
80		54
71		17
26		83
35		60
91		55
47		63
39		41

2 Solve each number problem. Choose the correct symbol. = < >

10 - 2		8 + 4
....		....

9 - 3		7 + 3
....		....

10 + 10		16 - 1
....		....

15 - 9		3 + 3
....		....

Work it out

Add the ones together first. Then add the tens together.

1 Add the numbers together to solve each problem.

$$10 + 7$$ ☐

$$13 + 5$$ ☐

$$12 + 2$$ ☐

$$11 + 8$$ ☐

$$10 + 0$$ ☐

$$11 + 1$$ ☐

2 Solve each problem two ways.

$$22 + 6$$ ☐

$$26 + 3$$ ☐

$$30 + 5$$ ☐

$$35 + 4$$ ☐

$$33 + 3$$ ☐

$$38 + 1$$ ☐

Counting on, using a number line, and adding 10s and 1s are just some of the ways you could solve them.

22 + 6 = ...   26 + 3 = ...   30 + 5 = ...

35 + 4 = ...   33 + 3 = ...   38 + 1 = ...

Money and value

The **value** of a coin is how much it is worth.

1 Fill in the money fact file below.
The first one has been started for you.

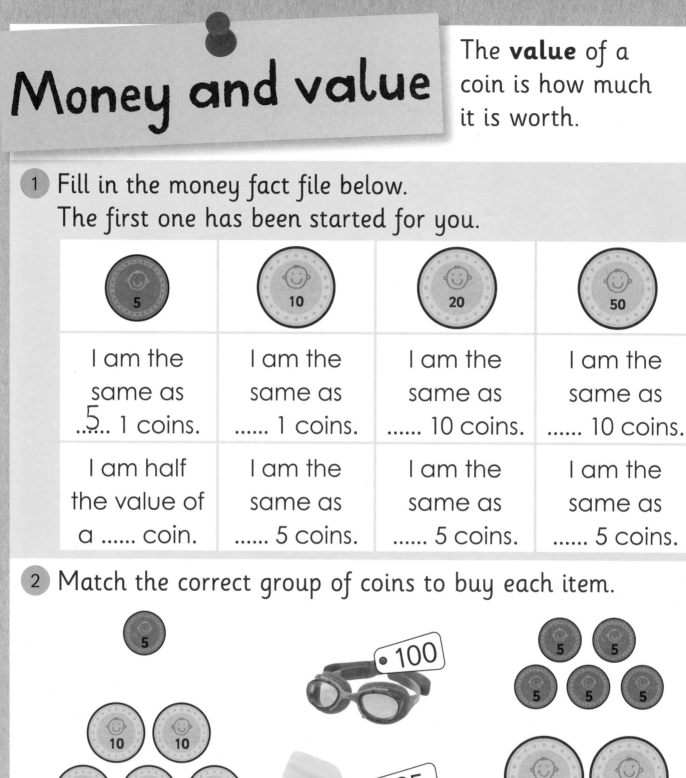

5	**10**	**20**	**50**
I am the same as ..5.. 1 coins.	I am the same as ...... 1 coins.	I am the same as ...... 10 coins.	I am the same as ...... 10 coins.
I am half the value of a ...... coin.	I am the same as ...... 5 coins.	I am the same as ...... 5 coins.	I am the same as ...... 5 coins.

2 Match the correct group of coins to buy each item.

There may be groups of coins left over!

104

Pocket money

Use your knowledge of the **value** of coins to buy the items shown below. You may need to add coins together.

1　Circle the coin, or coins, you need to buy each item.

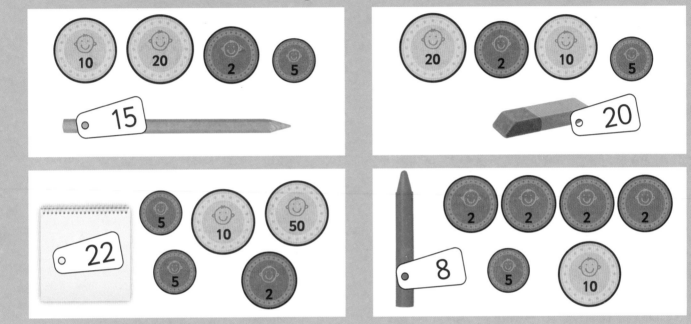

2　Circle the coins you need to buy each item.

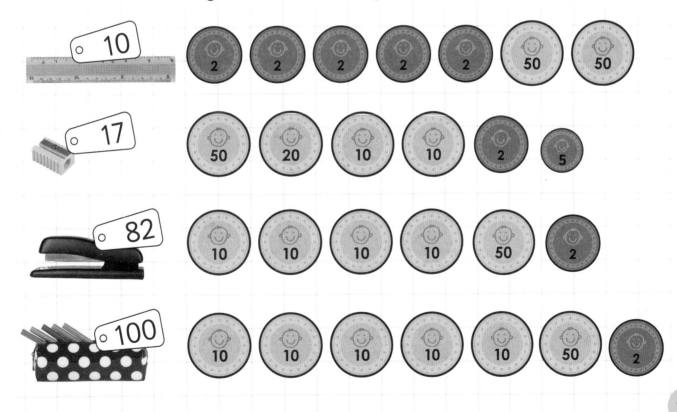

3D shape fact file

1 Fill in the missing information about the 3D shapes.

shape	name	faces	edges	vertices
	sphere	1	0	0

Cats and dogs problem solving

It's time to play detective! Cross out the animals as you read the clues.

1 Can you work out which puppy Buster is? Draw a circle around him.

| He is sitting down. | He has brown fur. | He is wearing a collar. |

a.   b.   c.   d.

2 Read the clues to work out which kitten Mittens is, then draw a circle around her.

| She is standing up. | She does not have stripy fur. | Her fur is gray. |

a.   b.   c.   d.

How much?

1 Draw a line between each item and the correct group of coins you will need to buy it.

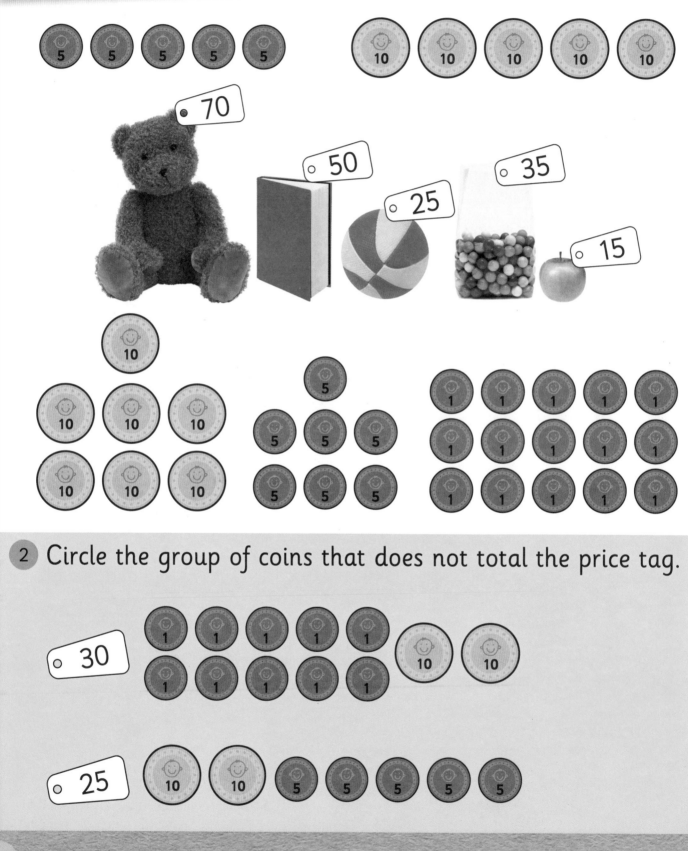

2 Circle the group of coins that does not total the price tag.

Measure using inches

An **inch** is a unit of measurement.

This is the actual size of an inch!

1 inch

A ruler is 12 inches long.

1. Decide if each tiny toy instrument is less than 1 inch or more than 1 inch long. Circle your answer below each item.

| < 1 inch | < 1 inch | < 1 inch | < 1 inch |
| > 1 inch | > 1 inch | > 1 inch | > 1 inch |

2. Use a ruler to measure each object.

The banjo is .... inches long.

The harmonica is .... inches long.

The violin is .... inches long.

The flute is .... inches long.

Let's estimate

Estimating allows us to roughly calculate the value or quantity of something. We use estimates of numbers to make it easier to do quick calculations in our head.

1 Estimate how many items are in each group.
Then count the fruit to check your estimate answer.

Estimate: ....

Count check: ....

Estimate: ....

Count check: ....

Estimate: ....

Count check: ....

2 Estimate how many candies are in each jar, then count them and draw a line to match each jar to the correct amount.

| 23 | 8 | 14 |

Volume

Volume tells us all about how much space an object takes up. Some containers can hold much more volume than others.

1 Many objects can be used to hold volume, such as a cup or watering can. Circle the objects you would use to hold a certain volume of something.

2 Circle the container in each pair that can hold more.

Nearly full and nearly empty

Volume tells us how much a container can hold.

nearly full	full	empty	nearly empty
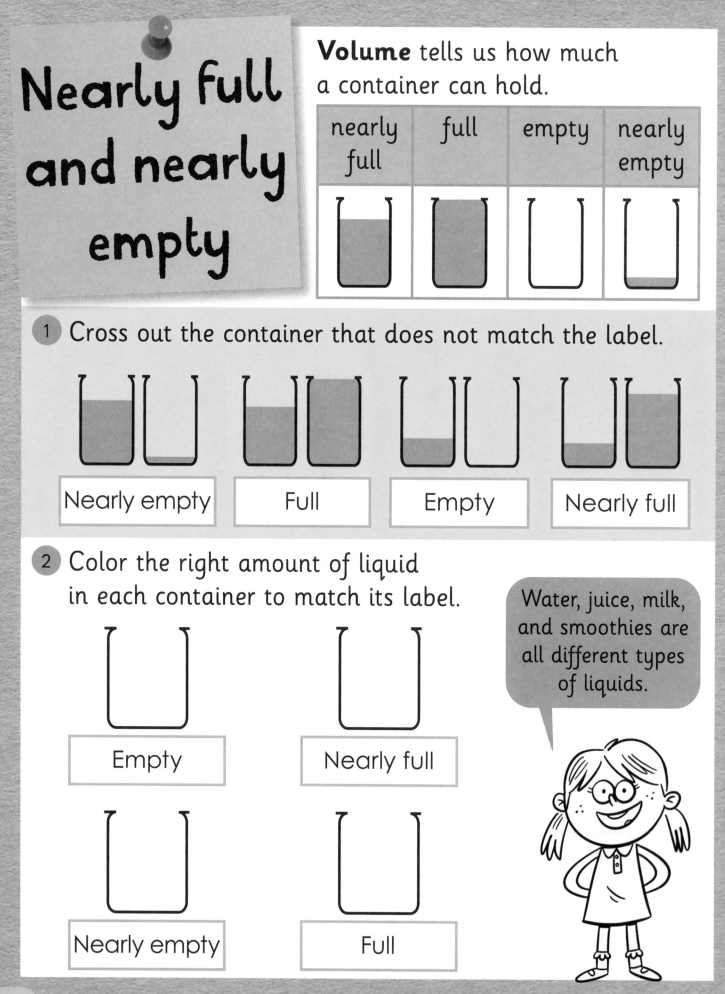			

1 Cross out the container that does not match the label.

Nearly empty   Full   Empty   Nearly full

2 Color the right amount of liquid in each container to match its label.

Empty

Nearly full

Nearly empty

Full

Water, juice, milk, and smoothies are all different types of liquids.

Class schedule time

Knowing what **time** it is helps us to plan our day and to know what to expect.

What time does school start? ....

1 Draw a line to match the times with the correct clock.

| 8 o'clock | Half past 1 | Half past 11 |

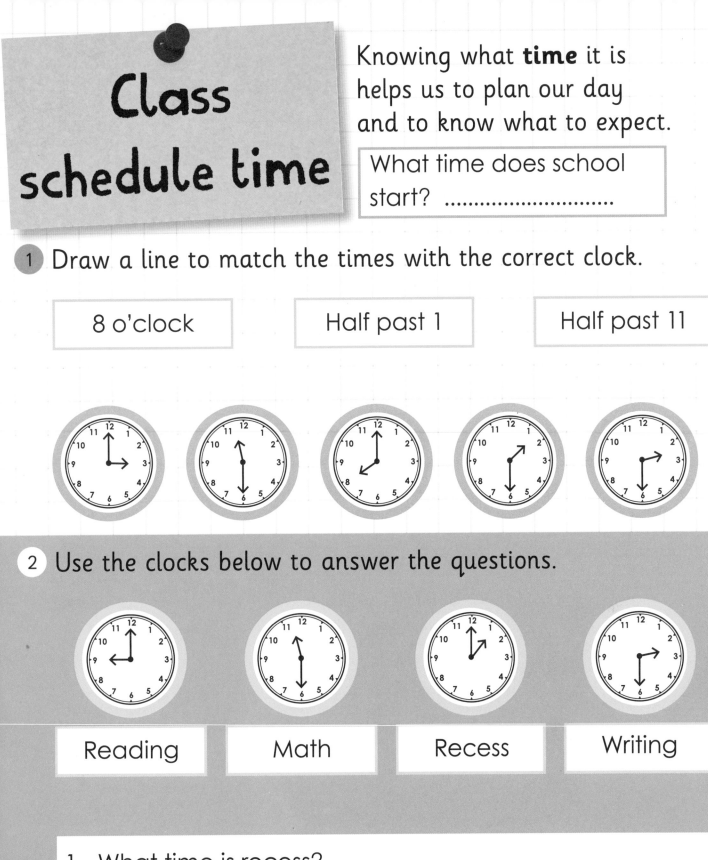

2 Use the clocks below to answer the questions.

Reading   Math   Recess   Writing

1. What time is recess? ....
2. When is it time for writing? ....
3. What happens first, math, or reading? ....
4. What time does math begin? ....

Number patterns

Use your **skip counting** knowledge to sort groups of numbers.

1 Sort the numbers from smallest value to biggest value.

a.
80		70	
	60		10
30		20	
	50		40

b.
16 6
12
20 18 8
4
10 2 14

a. ...., ..., ..., ..., ..., ..., ..., ...

b. ...., ..., ..., ..., ..., ..., ..., ..., ..., ...

2 There is a number missing in each of the jumps to 50.

Begin at 0. Count in jumps of 5. Circle each number as you say it. Find the missing number!

30   15   20   45   25   5   0   10   40   50

The missing number is ....

Begin at 0. Count in jumps of 2. Circle each number as you say it. Find the missing number!

32   40   8   34   20   44   18   6   30   4   22   16

24   46   0   2   10   36   14   38   12   50   26   28   42

The missing number is ....

Number chain to 100

1 Fill in the missing numbers.

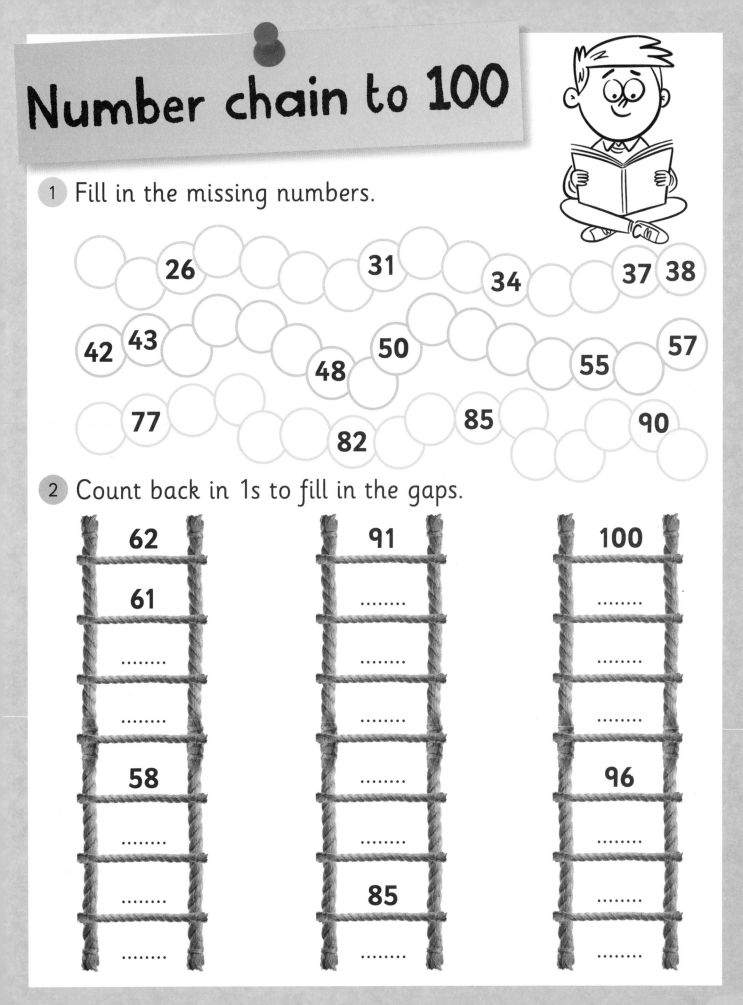

26   31   34   37 38

42 43   50   48   55 57

77   82   85   90

2 Count back in 1s to fill in the gaps.

62	91	100
61	....	....
....	....	....
....	....	....
58	....	96
....	....	....
....	85	....
....	....	....

100 square jumble

1. Fill in the missing digit in each of the numbers.

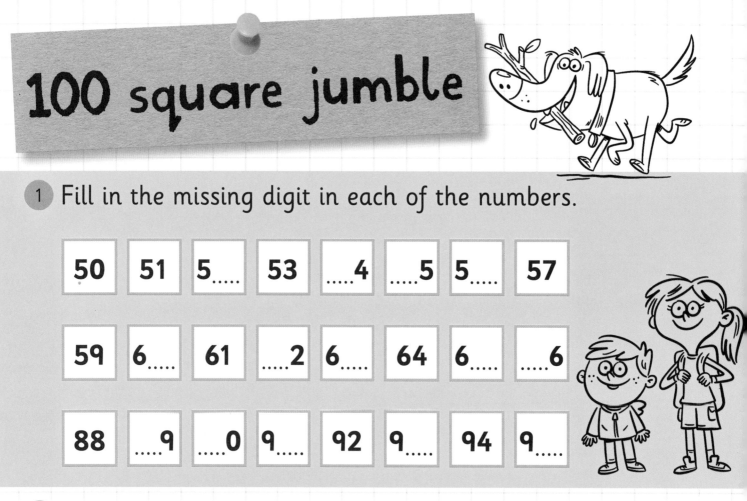

50	51	5....	53	4	5	5....	57
59	6....	61	2	6....	64	6....	6
88	9	0	9....	92	9....	94	9....

2. The 100 square is all jumbled up! Can you fill in the missing numbers to complete it again?

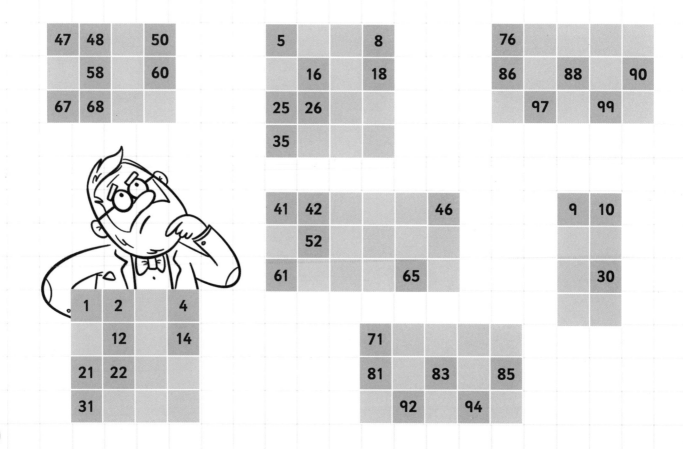

47	48		50
	58		60
67	68		

5			8
	16		18
25	26		
35			

76			
86		88		90
	97		99

41	42				46
	52				
61				65	

9	10
	30

1	2		4
	12		14
21	22		
31			

71				
81		83		85
	92		94	

116

The Queens' crowns

Challenge! You will need your thinking crown to solve this problem and answer the questions.

1 There should be one green, orange, red, and blue crown in each group. Circle the full group of crowns in each row.

2 Use the crowns above to answer the questions below.

1. How many groups are there altogether? ....

2. How many crowns are in each group? ....

3. If two green crowns were removed, how many full groups of crowns would there be? ....

Answers

Page 4-5

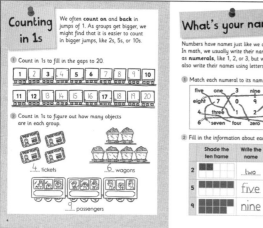

Page 6-7

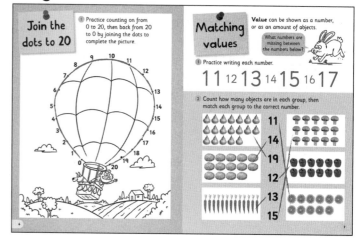

Page 8-9

Page 10-11

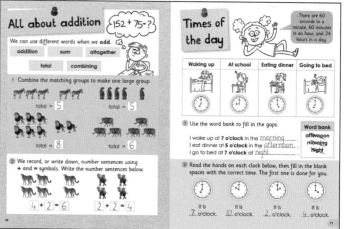

Page 12-13

Page 14-15

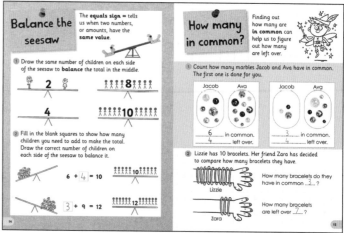

Page 16-17

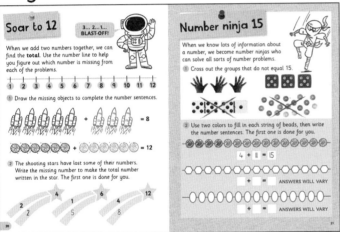

Find out the difference

Finding out the **difference** between two amounts tells us what information we need to include in a number sentence.

1 What is the difference between six and three?

$6 - 3 = 3$

You can use your fingers to solve the problem, like this:

2 Use your fingers to solve each subtraction problem below.

$10 - 5 = 5$ $8 - 3 = 5$ $7 - 2 = 5$

3 Count the objects and figure out how many more and less there are.

There are 7 🚤 and 4 ⛵

There are 3 more 🚤 than ⛵

There are 3 fewer ⛵ than 🚤

10 out of 10

Use your knowledge of 10 to solve the problems on this page.

1 Use the ten frames to help you solve each word problem.

Kylie had **10** apples. She kept **4** apples and gave the rest to Joe. How many apples did Joe get? 6

Ahmed shared his **10** apples equally with Ben. Ben got **5** apples. How many apples did Ahmed keep? 5

Sam found **10** apples. She gave **2** to Jen and kept the rest. How many apples did Sam get? 8

2 There are two parts to each word problem. Fill in the ten frame, then write the number sentence.

Draw 6 on the ten frame.		$6 + 4 = 10$
Draw 7 on the ten frame.		$7 + 3 = 10$
Draw 8 on the ten frame.		$8 + 2 = 10$

Page 18-19

Patterns all around

Patterns are all around us. We see them on our clothes, in our food, and even in math!

A **repeated** pattern is something that happens over and over again.

1 Can you figure out what comes next? Complete the patterns.

2 Using three colors, see how many flag patterns you can create by filling in each stripe in a different color.

ANSWERS WILL VARY

Pattern creator

We can check if a **sequence** is a repeating pattern by seeing if it follows the same rule over and over again. If the sequence does not follow the same rule over and over again, it is not a repeating pattern.

3 Circle the sequences that have repeating patterns.

2 Create three different repeating patterns using the following shapes:

How many repeating patterns can you make from these shapes?

Pattern 1:
.... ANSWERS WILL VARY

Pattern 2:
.... ANSWERS WILL VARY

Pattern 3:
.... ANSWERS WILL VARY

Page 20-21

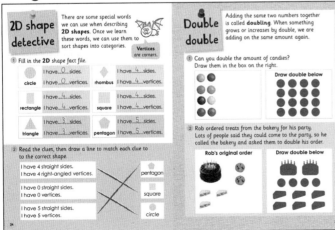

Soar to 12

3... 2...1... BLAST-OFF!

When we add two numbers together, we can find the **total**. Use the number line to help you figure out which number is missing from each of the problems.

1 2 3 4 5 6 7 8 9 10 11 12

1 Draw the missing objects to complete the number sentences.

🚀🚀 + 🚀🚀🚀🚀🚀 = 8

+ = 12

2 The shooting stars have lost some of their numbers. Write the missing number to make the total number written in the star. The first one is done for you.

2 / 2   4 / 5   1   6 / 8   12

Number ninja 15

When we know lots of information about a number, we become number ninjas who can solve all sorts of number problems.

1 Cross out the groups that do not equal 15.

2 Use two colors to fill in each string of beads, then write the number sentences. The first one is done for you.

$4 + 11 = 15$

+ = ANSWERS WILL VARY

+ = ANSWERS WILL VARY

Page 22-23

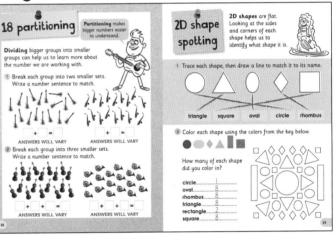

18 partitioning

Partitioning makes bigger numbers easier to understand.

Dividing bigger groups into smaller groups can help us to learn more about the number we are working with.

1 Break each group into two smaller sets. Write a number sentence to match.

+ = ANSWERS WILL VARY   + = ANSWERS WILL VARY

2 Break each group into three smaller sets. Write a number sentence to match.

+ + = ANSWERS WILL VARY   + + = ANSWERS WILL VARY

2D shape spotting

2D shapes are flat. Looking at the sides and corners of each shape helps us to identify what shape it is.

1 Trace each shape, then draw a line to match it to its name.

triangle   square   oval   circle   rhombus

2 Color each shape using the colors from the key below.

How many of each shape did you color in?

circle 8
oval 8
rhombus 8
triangle 8
rectangle 2
square 8

Page 24-25

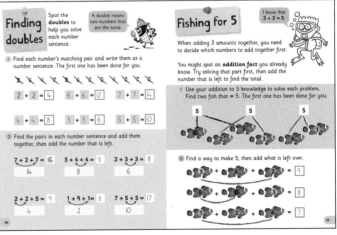

2D shape detective

There are some special words we can use when describing **2D shapes**. Once we learn these words, we can use them to sort shapes into categories.

Vertices are corners.

1 Fill in the 2D shape fact file.

circle — I have 0 sides. I have 0 vertices.	rhombus — I have 4 sides. I have 4 vertices.	
rectangle — I have 4 sides. I have 4 vertices.	square — I have 4 sides. I have 4 vertices.	
triangle — I have 3 sides. I have 3 vertices.	pentagon — I have 5 sides. I have 5 vertices.	

2 Read the clues, then draw a line to match each clue to to the correct shape.

I have 4 straight sides. I have 4 right-angled vertices. → pentagon

I have 0 straight sides. I have 0 vertices. → square

I have 5 straight sides. I have 5 vertices. → circle

Double double

Adding the same two numbers together is called **doubling**. When something grows or increases by double, we are adding on the same amount again.

1 Can you double the amount of candies? Draw them in the box on the right.

Draw double below

2 Rob ordered treats from the bakery for his party. Lots of people said they could come to the party, so he called the bakery and asked them to double his order.

Rob's original order   Draw double below

Page 26-27

Finding doubles

Spot the **doubles** to help you solve each number sentence.

A double means two numbers that are the same.

1 Find each number's matching pair and write them as a number sentence. The first one has been done for you.

$2 + 2 = 4$ $6 + 6 = 12$ $7 + 7 = 14$

$4 + 4 = 8$ $3 + 3 = 6$ $5 + 5 = 10$

2 Find the pairs in each number sentence and add them together, then add the number that is left.

$7 + 2 + 7 = 16$ $3 + 4 + 4 = 11$ $2 + 3 + 3 = 8$
  14   8   6

$2 + 2 + 5 = 9$ $1 + 9 + 1 = 11$ $7 + 5 + 5 = 17$
  4   2   10

Fishing for 5

I know that $3 + 2 = 5$.

When adding 3 amounts together, you need to decide which numbers to add together first.

You might spot an **addition fact** you already know. Try solving that part first, then add the number that is left to find the total.

1 Use your addition to 5 knowledge to solve each problem. Find two fish that = 5. The first one has been done for you.

5   5   5

2 Find a way to make 5, then add what is left over.

+ + = 9

+ + = 8

+ + = 7

Answers

Page 28-29

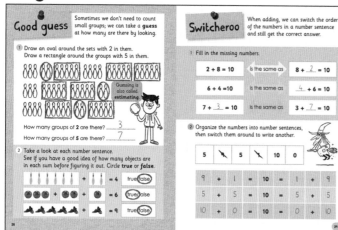

Page 30-31

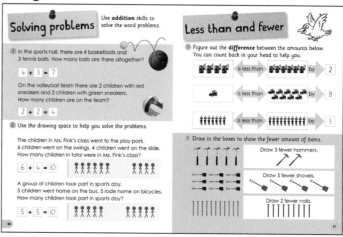

Page 32-33

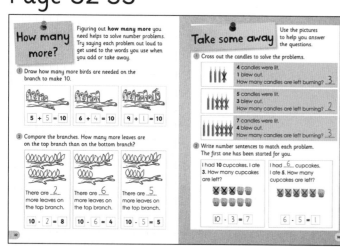

Page 34-35

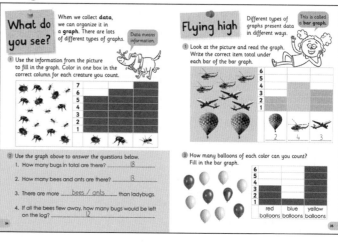

Page 36-37

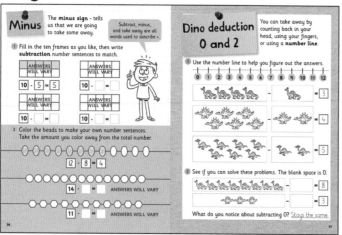

Page 38-39

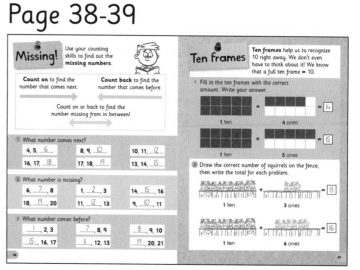

Page 40-41

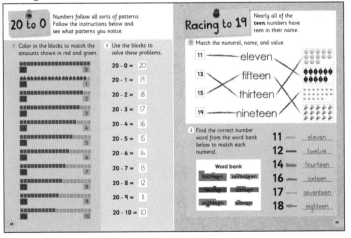

Page 42-43

Page 44-45

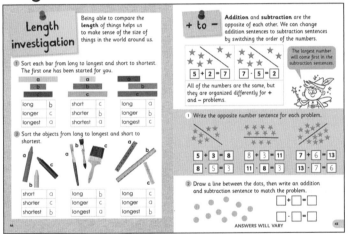

Page 46-47

Page 48-49

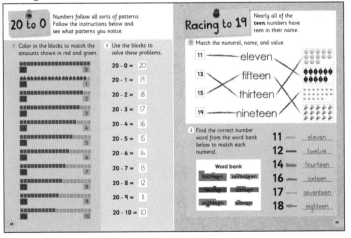

Page 50-51

Answers

Page 52-53

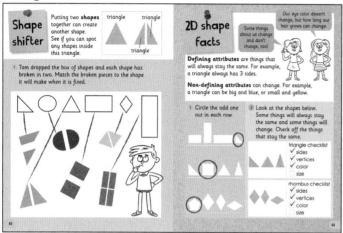

Page 54-55

Page 56-57

Page 58-59

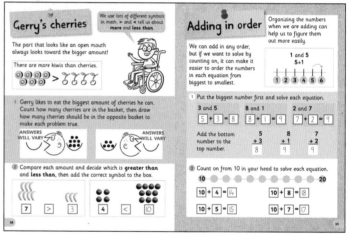

Page 60-61

Page 62-63

Page 64-65

Build an odd and even wall

① Solve the problem in each brick. When you are finished, circle the answers that are **even** numbers.

$5 + 8 = 13$	$11 + 3 = 14$	$6 + 6 = 12$
$4 + 6 = 10$	$8 + 7 = 15$	$9 + 1 = 10$
$13 + 7 = 20$	$17 + 2 = 19$	$9 + 9 = 18$
$9 + 10 = 19$	$9 + 8 = 16$	$12 + 5 = 17$

② Count in 2s to fill in the missing numbers.

Even sequences:
4 6 8 10 12 14
12 14 16 18 20 22

Odd sequences:
3 5 7 9 11 13
13 15 17 19 21 23

Sharing in half

When we divide something in **half**, we share it into **two equal parts**.

① Annie and her brother are sharing lunch. Color in Annie's half of the food.

② ✓ Check the items that have been shared equally.
✗ X the items that have not been shared equally.

Page 66-67

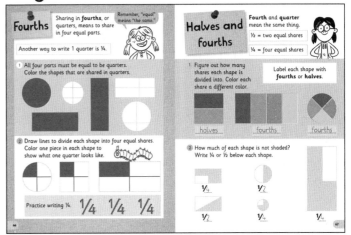

Fourths

Sharing in **fourths**, or quarters, means to share in four equal parts.

Remember, "equal" means "the same".

Another way to write 1 quarter is ¼.

① All four parts must be equal to be quarters. Color the shapes that are shared in quarters.

② Draw lines to divide each shape into four equal shares. Color one piece each shape to show what one quarter looks like.

Practice writing ¼.   ¼ ¼ ¼

Halves and fourths

Fourth and **quarter** mean the same thing.
½ = two equal shares
¼ = four equal shares

① Figure out how many shares each shape is divided into. Color each share a different color.

Label each shape with **fourths** or **halves**.

halves   fourths   fourths

② How much of each shape is not shaded? Write ¼ or ½ below each shape.

¼   ½
½   ¼   ¼

Page 68-69

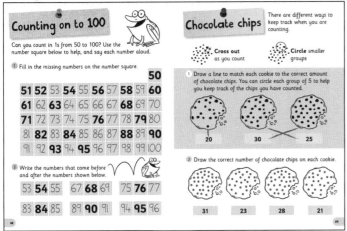

Counting on to 100

Can you count in 1s from 50 to 100? Use the number square below to help, and say each number aloud.

① Fill in the missing numbers on the number square.

| 50 |
51	52	53	54	55	56	57	58	59	60
61	62	63	64	65	66	67	68	69	70
71	72	73	74	75	76	77	78	79	80
81	82	83	84	85	86	87	88	89	90
91	92	93	94	95	96	97	98	99	100

② Write the numbers that come before and after the numbers shown below.

53 54 55   67 68 69   75 76 77
83 84 85   89 90 91   94 95 96

Chocolate chips

There are different ways to keep track when you are counting.

Cross out as you count
Circle smaller groups

① Draw a line to match each cookie to the correct amount of chocolate chips. You can circle each group of 5 to help you keep track of the chips you have counted.

20   30   25

② Draw the correct number of chocolate chips on each cookie.

31   23   28   21

Page 70-71

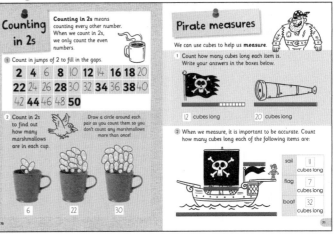

Counting in 2s

Counting in 2s means counting every other number. When we count in 2s, we only count the even numbers.

① Count in jumps of 2 to fill in the gaps.

2 4 6 8 10 12 14 16 18 20
22 24 26 28 30 32 34 36 38 40
42 44 46 48 50

② Count in 2s to find out how many marshmallows are in each cup.

Draw a circle around each pair as you count them so you don't count any marshmallows more than once!

6   22   30

Pirate measures

We can use cubes to help us **measure**.

① Count how many cubes long each item is. Write your answers in the boxes below.

12 cubes long   20 cubes long

② When we measure, it is important to be accurate. Count how many cubes long each of the following items are:

sail — 11 cubes long
flag — 7 cubes long
boat — 32 cubes long

Page 72-73

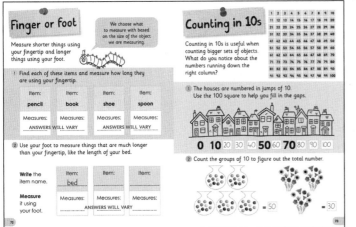

Finger or foot

We choose what to measure with based on the size of the object we are measuring.

Measure shorter things using your fingertip and longer things using your foot.

① Find each of these items and measure how long they are using your fingertip.

| Item: pencil | Item: book | Item: shoe | Item: spoon |
| Measures: ANSWERS WILL VARY | Measures: ANSWERS WILL VARY | Measures: | Measures: |

② Use your foot to measure things that are much longer than your fingertip, like the length of your bed.

Write the item name. — Item: bed
Measure it using your foot. — Measures: ANSWERS WILL VARY

Counting in 10s

Counting in 10s is useful when counting bigger sets of objects. What do you notice about the numbers running down the right column?

1	2	3	4	5	6	7	8	9	10
11	12	13	14	15	16	17	18	19	20
21	22	23	24	25	26	27	28	29	30
31	32	33	34	35	36	37	38	39	40
41	42	43	44	45	46	47	48	49	50
51	52	53	54	55	56	57	58	59	60
61	62	63	64	65	66	67	68	69	70
71	72	73	74	75	76	77	78	79	80
81	82	83	84	85	86	87	88	89	90
91	92	93	94	95	96	97	98	99	100

① The houses are numbered in jumps of 10. Use the 100 square to help you fill in the gaps.

0 10 20 30 40 50 60 70 80 90 100

② Count the groups of 10 to figure out the total number.

= 50   = 30

Page 74-75

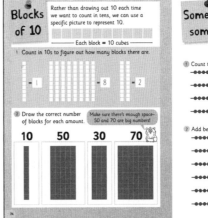

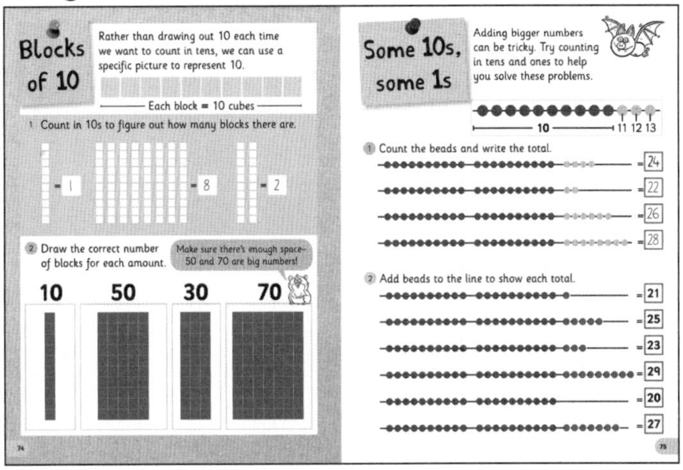

Blocks of 10

Rather than drawing out 10 each time we want to count in tens, we can use a specific picture to represent 10.

— Each block = 10 cubes —

① Count in 10s to figure out how many blocks there are.

= 1   = 8   = 2

② Draw the correct number of blocks for each amount.

Make sure there's enough space—50 and 70 are big numbers!

10   50   30   70

Some 10s, some 1s

Adding bigger numbers can be tricky. Try counting in tens and ones to help you solve these problems.

10   11 12 13

① Count the beads and write the total.

24
22
26
28

② Add beads to the line to show each total.

21
25
23
29
20
27

Answers

Page 76-77

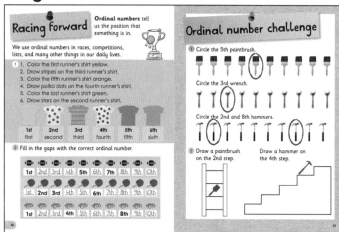

Page 78-79

Page 80-81

Page 82-83

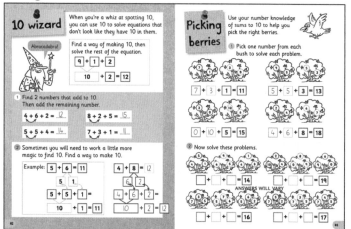

Page 84-85

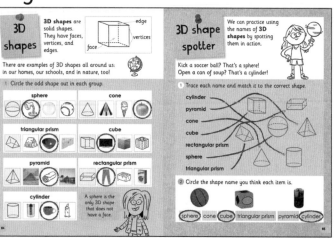

Page 86-87

Page 88-89

Page 90-91

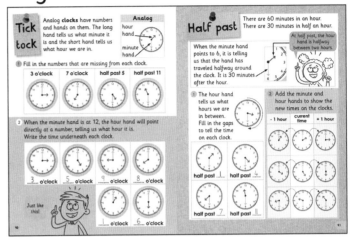

Page 92-93

Page 94-95

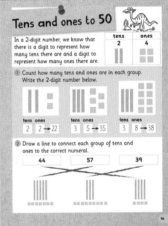

Page 96-97

Page 98-99

Answers

Page 100-101

Ordering numbers

Order numbers by **counting on** or **counting back**.

If you can count to 100, you can order numbers to 100!

① Count in ones to fill in the gaps on the flags.

15 | 16 | 17 | 18 | 19 | 20 | 21 | 22 | 23 | 24

40 | 41 | 42 | 43 | 44 | 45 | 46 | 47 | 48 | 49

67 | 68 | 69 | 70 | 71 | 72 | 73 | 74 | 75 | 76

② Count on and back in 2s and 5s to fill the gaps.

-2		+2	
42	44	30	32
70	72	58	60
84	86	92	94

-5		+5	
60	65	75	80
75	80	90	95
40	45	30	35

Number line hop to 99

Use your number knowledge to solve each challenge.

① Begin at 28. Jump forward 2. What number did you land on? 30.

28 | 29 | 30

Begin at 47. Jump forward 5. What number did you land on? 52.

47 | 48 | 49 | 50 | 51 | 52

Begin at 80. Jump back 6. What number did you land on? 74.

74 | 75 | 76 | 77 | 78 | 79 | 80

② Read the clues to figure out the correct number. Use the 100 square to help.

I am 10 less than 69. I am 59.

I have 5 tens and the same number of ones. I am 55.

I am 20 more than 71. I am 91.

I have 7 tens. I have more than 8 ones. I am 79.

Page 102-103

Greater than, less than, equal

We use symbols to show when a number or equation is **greater than, less than,** or **equal to**.

>	<	=
greater than	less than	equal to

① Compare the numbers. Decide which symbol tells you about each pair. < >

14	<	21
80	>	54
71	>	17
26	<	83
35	<	60
91	>	55
47	<	63
39	<	41

② Solve each number problem. Choose the correct symbol. = < >

10 - 2		8 + 4
8	<	12
9 - 3		7 + 3
6	<	10
10 + 10		16 - 1
20	>	15
15 - 9		3 + 3
6	=	6

Work it out

Add the ones together first. Then add the tens together.

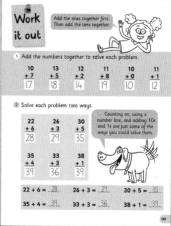

① Add the numbers together to solve each problem.

| 10 +7 = 17 | 13 +5 = 18 | 12 +2 = 14 | 11 +8 = 19 | 10 +0 = 10 | 11 +1 = 12 |

② Solve each problem two ways.

Counting on, using a number line, and adding 10s and 1s are just some of the ways you could solve them.

| 22 +6 = 28 | 26 +3 = 29 | 30 +5 = 35 |
| 35 +4 = 39 | 33 +3 = 36 | 38 +1 = 39 |

22 + 6 = 28   26 + 3 = 29   30 + 5 = 35

35 + 4 = 39   33 + 3 = 36   38 + 1 = 39

Page 104-105

Money and value

The **value** of a coin is how much it is worth.

① Fill in the money fact file below. The first one has been started for you.

I am the same as 5 1 coins.
I am the same as 10 1 coins.
I am the same as 2 10 coins.
I am the same as 2 10 coins.

I am half the value of a 10 coin.
I am the same as 2 5 coins.
I am the same as 4 5 coins.
I am the same as 10 5 coins.

② Match the correct group of coins to buy each item.

There may be groups of coins left over!

Pocket money

Use your knowledge of the **value** of coins to buy the items shown below. You may need to add coins together.

① Circle the coin, or coins, you need to buy each item.

15   20   22   8

② Circle the coins you need to buy each item.

10   17   82   100

Page 106-107

3D shape fact file

① Fill in the missing information about the 3D shapes.

shape	name	faces	edges	vertices
	sphere	1	0	0
	cube	6	12	8
	cone	2	1	1
	triangular prism	5	9	6
	square based pyramid	5	8	5
	cylinder	3	2	0
	rectangular prism	6	12	8

Cats and dogs problem solving

It's time to play detective! Cross out the animals as you read the clues.

① Can you work out which puppy Buster is? Draw a circle around him.

He is sitting down.   He has brown fur.   He is wearing a collar.

② Read the clues to work out which kitten Mittens is, then draw a circle around her.

She is standing up.   She does not have stripy fur.   Her fur is gray.

Page 108-109

How much?

① Draw a line between each item and the correct group of coins you will need to buy it.

70   50   25   35   15

② Circle the group of coins that does not total the price tag.

30   25

Measure using inches

An **inch** is a unit of measurement.

This is the actual size of an inch!

1 inch

A ruler is 12 inches long.

① Decide if each tiny toy instrument is less than 1 inch or more than 1 inch long. Circle your answer below each item.

< 1 inch | < 1 inch | < 1 inch | < 1 inch
> 1 inch | > 1 inch | > 1 inch | > 1 inch

② Use a ruler to measure each object.

The banjo is 2.5 inches long.

The harmonica is 1.5 inches long.

The violin is 2 inches long.

The flute is 2.5 inches long.

Page 110-111

Let's estimate

Estimating allows us to roughly calculate the value or quantity of something. We use estimates of numbers to make it easier to do quick calculations in our head.

① Estimate how many items are in each group. Then count the fruit to check your estimate answer.

Estimate: ...   Estimate: ...   Estimate: ...
Count check: 6   Count check: 12   Count check: 20

*ANSWERS WILL VARY

② Estimate how many candies are in each jar, then count them and draw a line to match each jar to the correct amount.

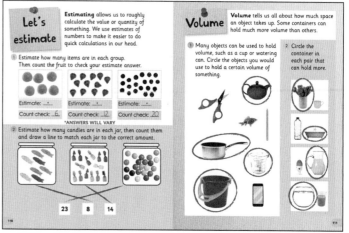

23   8   14

Volume

Volume tells us all about how much space an object takes up. Some containers can hold much more volume than others.

① Many objects can be used to hold volume, such as a cup or watering can. Circle the objects you would use to hold a certain volume of something.

② Circle the container in each pair that can hold more.

Page 112-113

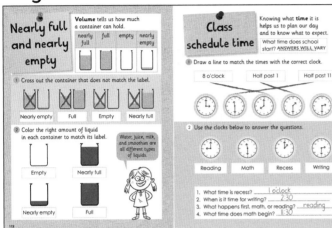

Nearly full and nearly empty

Volume tells us how much a container can hold.

nearly full | full | empty | nearly empty

① Cross out the container that does not match the label.

Nearly empty | Full | Empty | Nearly full

② Color the right amount of liquid in each container to match its label.

Empty | Nearly full

Nearly empty | Full

Water, juice, milk, and smoothies are all different types of liquids.

Class schedule time

Knowing what **time** it is helps us to plan our day and to know what to expect.

What time does school start? ANSWERS WILL VARY

① Draw a line to match the times with the correct clock.

8 o'clock | Half past 1 | Half past 11

② Use the clocks below to answer the questions.

Reading | Math | Recess | Writing

1. What time is recess? _1 o'clock_
2. When is it time for writing? _2:30_
3. What happens first, math, or reading? _reading_
4. What time does math begin? _11:30_

Page 114-115

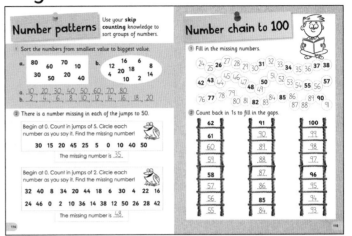

Number patterns

Use your **skip counting** knowledge to sort groups of numbers.

① Sort the numbers from smallest value to biggest value.

a. 80 60 70 10 30 50 20 40
b. 12 16 6 8 4 20 18 10 2 14

a. _10, 20, 30, 40, 50, 60, 70, 80_
b. _2, 4, 6, 8, 10, 12, 14, 16, 18, 20_

② There is a number missing in each of the jumps to 50.

Begin at 0. Count in jumps of 5. Circle each number as you say it. Find the missing number!

30 15 20 45 25 5 0 10 40 50

The missing number is _35_.

Begin at 0. Count in jumps of 2. Circle each number as you say it. Find the missing number!

32 40 8 34 20 44 18 6 30 4 22 16
24 46 0 2 10 36 14 38 12 50 26 28 42

The missing number is _48_.

Number chain to 100

① Fill in the missing numbers.

24 25 26 27 28 29 30 31 32 33 34 35 36 37 38
42 43 44 45 46 47 48 49 50 51 52 53 54 55 56 57
76 77 78 79 80 81 82 83 84 85 86 87 88 89 90 91

② Count back in 1s to fill in the gaps.

62	91	100
61	90	99
60	89	98
59	88	97
58	87	96
57	86	95
56	85	94
55	84	93

Page 116-117

100 square jumble

① Fill in the missing digit in each of the numbers.

50 51 52 53 54 55 56 57
59 60 61 62 63 64 65 66
88 89 90 91 92 93 94 95

② The 100 square is all jumbled up! Can you fill in the missing numbers to complete it again?

47 48 49 50
57 58 59 60
67 68 69 70

5 6 7 8
15 16 17 18
25 26 27 28
35 36 37 38

76 77 78 79 80
86 87 88 89 90
96 97 98 99 100

1 2 3 4

41 42 43 44 45 46
51 52 53 54 55 56
61 62 63 64 65 66

9 10
19 20
29 30
39 40

11 12 13 14
21 22 23 24
31 32 33 34

71 72 73 74 75
81 82 83 84 85
91 92 93 94 95

The Queens' crowns

Challenge! You will need your thinking crown to solve this problem and answer the questions.

① There should be one green, orange, red, and blue crown in each group. Circle the full group of crowns in each row.

② Use the crowns above to answer the questions below.

1. How many groups are there altogether? _3_
2. How many crowns are in each group? _4_
3. If two green crowns were removed, how many full groups of crowns would there be? _____

Credits

Educational Consultants: Kimberley Burnim & Ciara O'Conner, BEd, MA
Editors: Alice-May Bermingham & Natalia Boileau
Senior Designer: Rhea Gaughan
Designer: Nic Davies & Alice Baird
Production Controller: Rosie Cunniffe
Illustrator: Lee Cosgrove